T0302417

HBR Guide to **Work-Life Balance**

Harvard Business Review Guides

Arm yourself with the advice you need to succeed on the job, from the most trusted brand in business. Packed with how-to essentials from leading experts, the HBR Guides provide smart answers to your most pressing work challenges.

The titles include:

HBR Guide to Being More Productive
HBR Guide to Better Business Writing
HBR Guide to Building Your Business Case
HBR Guide to Buying a Small Business
HBR Guide to Coaching Employees
HBR Guide to Data Analytics Basics for Managers
HBR Guide to Delivering Effective Feedback
HBR Guide to Emotional Intelligence
HBR Guide to Finance Basics for Managers
HBR Guide to Getting the Right Work Done
HBR Guide to Leading Teams
HBR Guide to Making Every Meeting Matter
HBR Guide to Managing Stress at Work
HBR Guide to Managing Up and Across
HBR Guide to Negotiating
HBR Guide to Office Politics
HBR Guide to Performance Management
HBR Guide to Persuasive Presentations
HBR Guide to Project Management

HBR Guide to
Work-Life Balance

HARVARD BUSINESS REVIEW PRESS

Boston, Massachusetts

HBR Press Quantity Sales Discounts

Harvard Business Review Press titles are available at significant quantity discounts when purchased in bulk for client gifts, sales promotions, and premiums. Special editions, including books with corporate logos, customized covers, and letters from the company or CEO printed in the front matter, as well as excerpts of existing books, can also be created in large quantities for special needs.

For details and discount information for both print and ebook formats, contact booksales@harvardbusiness.org, tel. 800-988-0886, or www.hbr.org/bulksales.

Copyright 2019 Harvard Business School Publishing Corporation

All rights reserved

Printed in the United States of America

10 9 8 7 6 5 4 3 2 1

No part of this publication may be reproduced, stored in or introduced into a retrieval system, or transmitted, in any form, or by any means (electronic, mechanical, photocopying, recording, or otherwise), without the prior permission of the publisher. Requests for permission should be directed to permissions@hbsp.harvard.edu, or mailed to Permissions, Harvard Business School Publishing, 60 Harvard Way, Boston, Massachusetts 02163.

The web addresses referenced in this book were live and correct at the time of the book's publication but may be subject to change.

Library of Congress Cataloging-in-Publication Data

Title: HBR guide to work-life balance.
Other titles: Harvard Business Review guide to work-life balance | Work-life balance | Harvard business review guides.
Description: Boston, Massachusetts : Harvard Business Review Press, [2019] | Series: Harvard business review guides
Identifiers: LCCN 2018049545 | ISBN 9781633697126 (pbk.)
Subjects: LCSH: Work-life balance. | Quality of Life. | Work and family.
Classification: LCC HD4904.25 .H395 2019 | DDC 650.1—dc23
LC record available at https://lccn.loc.gov/2018049545

ISBN: 978-1-63369-712-6

eISBN: 978-1-63369-713-3

The paper used in this publication meets the requirements of the American National Standard for Permanence of Paper for Publications and Documents in Libraries and Archives Z39.48-1992

What You'll Learn

Must work and life always be at odds? It certainly seems that way, especially on those days where you run from one thing to the next but all you accomplish is feeling overextended and defeated. No matter your age, marital or parental status, or profession, you juggle a lot. Work, home, family duties, volunteer activities, your own interests and mental health—every day you face the constant push and pull of a full life.

But having a full life isn't a bad thing, and it doesn't have to be a constant source of stress. You'll never divide your time or attention evenly, but you can discover ways to set priorities and make trade-offs, so that you feel less stressed about them. This guide will help you manage your competing interests more effectively, with carefully selected advice from a variety of expert voices.

You'll learn how to:

- Contribute to the most important areas of your life without depleting your energy
- Identify and adjust where you're spending your time

- Establish a schedule that works for mostly everyone, most of the time
- Ease the guilt of saying no by recognizing it means saying yes to one of your priorities
- Transfer skills from one area of your life to another
- Create a business case for flexible work hours
- Manage expectations at home and at work
- Conduct difficult conversations when schedule conflicts crop up
- Protect your focus by setting boundaries
- Get more sleep

Contents

Introduction 1

SECTION ONE

Take Stock

1. Be a Better Leader, Have a Richer Life 7

Integrate the four domains of your life: work, home, community, self.

BY STEWART D. FRIEDMAN

2. Assessment: Are You Focusing on What's Important to You? 33

Where are you actually spending your time and attention?

BY STEWART D. FRIEDMAN

SECTION TWO

Make Decisions and Manage Your Time

3. No, You Can't Have It All 41

A framework for managing your toughest trade-offs.

BY ERIC C. SINOWAY

4. Make Room in Your Work Life for the Rest of Your Self 53

Manage your portfolio of identities.

BY BRIANNA CAZA, LAKSHMI RAMARAJAN, ERIN REID, AND STEPHANIE CREARY

5. Before You Agree to Take on New Work, Ask Three Questions 63

Shed your "shoulds."

BY REGAN WALSH

6. Stop Work Overload by Setting These Boundaries 73

Create a time budget and reclaim your life.

BY ELIZABETH GRACE SAUNDERS

7. Nine Practices to Help You Say No 83

Part of saying yes to the right things is learning to say no.

BY PETER BREGMAN

8. Why You Need an Untouchable Day Every Week 89

And how to get one.

BY NEIL PASRICHA

9. How to Get the Most Out of a Day Off 95

Take a micro-vacation with lasting benefits.

BY ELIZABETH GRACE SAUNDERS

SECTION THREE

Explore Flexible Work Arrangements

10. Winning Support for Flexible Work 103

Propose a schedule that benefits everyone.

BY AMY GALLO

11. Five Strategies of Successful Part-Time Work 111

Routines and rituals are key.

BY VIVIEN CORWIN, THOMAS B. LAWRENCE, AND PETER J. FROST

12. Staying Focused When You're Working from Home 131

Set "office hours"—and stick to them.

BY ELIZABETH GRACE SAUNDERS

13. What to Do When a Personal Crisis Is Hurting Your Professional Life 137

From dealing with illness to managing a divorce.

BY AMY GALLO

SECTION FOUR

Manage Your Relationships

14. Being Too Busy for Friends Won't Help Your Career 147

Success starts with a foundation of strong, stable friendships.

BY NEAL J. ROESE

15. Two-Career Couples Need Long-Term Plans 153

Make arrangements and stay flexible.

BY AVIVAH WITTENBERG-COX

16. Balance Parenting and Work Stress 161
Manage the greatest challenges head-on.
BY DAISY WADEMAN DOWLING

17. How Working Parents Can Manage the Demands of School-Age Kids 169
Control the chaos.
BY DAISY WADEMAN DOWLING

18. Keep Your Home Life Sane When Work Gets Crazy 177
Communicate with the people who matter most.
BY STEWART D. FRIEDMAN

SECTION FIVE

Take Care of Yourself

19. Six Ways to Weave Self-Care into Your Workday 185
It's not a luxury; it's a job requirement.
BY AMY JEN SU

20. The Difference Between Workaholics and Working Long Hours 193
. . . is about your approach, not about time.
BY LIEKE TEN BRUMMELHUIS AND NANCY P. ROTHBARD

21. How to Forget About Work When You're Not Working 209
Develop new habits.
BY ART MARKMAN

22. Regular Exercise Is Part of Your Job 215

Work it out.

BY RON FRIEDMAN

23. Reclaim Your Commute 221

Five tweaks to try.

BY FRANCESCA GINO, BRADLEY STAATS, JON JACHIMOWICZ, JULIA LEE, AND JOCHEN MENGES

24. Get Better Sleep 231

How you spend the last 10 minutes of your day matters.

BY RON FRIEDMAN

25. Don't Take a Bad Day Home with You 237

Leave on a high note.

BY JOHN BALDONI

Index 239

Introduction

If time and energy were infinite, we could fulfill our commitments without losing our minds. We could deliver that keynote address at our industry's largest conference and clap the loudest at the third-grade recorder concert halfway around the world. We could give back to our community by chairing a fundraiser to end food insecurity for families without shirking the requisite late nights that lead up to closing out the month-end process. We could commit to our health and train for a marathon with impunity, even when it means blocking off meeting-free spaces in our calendars to accommodate long runs and showers.

But we are painfully aware that time and energy are finite and that there doesn't appear to be one magic fix. In fact, the advice on juggling the components of our lives is conflicting. You can have it all. No, you can't have it all, writes Eric Sinoway (entrepreneur and contributor to this volume). Balance your work and life. "Balance is bunk," declares work-life integration expert (and contributor to this volume) Stewart Friedman. To honor our commitments and not collapse from exhaustion, we must find ways to integrate the many aspects of our lives. To take in the conflicting advice, try some of the recommended approaches. Adopt what works for you and abandon what doesn't to weave your personal and professional identities into some semblance of a whole—a whole that is not frazzled or pulled in a thousand directions. Work-life balance may be bunk, but it doesn't have to be a knockdown, drag-out competition, either.

When you accept that you can't do it all, you can make deliberate choices about the life you want to lead. You can manage expectations. You can set boundaries. You can carve out focused time for important work. You can stop talking about self-care and actually practice it. Your priorities will become clear. This guide will help ease the tension you're experiencing between the segments of your life by offering a variety of approaches—some grounded in research, some born of practice.

Who This Book Is For

If this book is in your hands, it's for you. This guide is for anyone struggling to make room for all of the components that come together to create our very busy—and very rich—lives.

It's for working parents and for those who are caring for elderly or ill family members. Whether you're in the early days of parenting and getting yanked out of a meeting to retrieve a feverish infant from daycare or in the later days of trying to find open slots in your double-booked schedule to take your kid on college tours, this book is for you. It's for people who want to get involved in local politics by making time to canvass or run for office. It's for people who want to volunteer their time to serve on boards and give back to organizations that matter to them. Perhaps you've just entered the workforce and the nine-to-five-plus routine has you frequently cancelling on your workout partner. Maybe you've achieved great success at work and are at the top of your organization but annoy your family because you just can't seem to be fully present at home. This book is for anyone who feels they may be shortchanging an area of their life that matters. Whether you know where you're falling behind or you can't quite figure out where you're neglecting your obligations, this book will help you refocus and reset your priorities. It offers practices for setting and spending your time budget. It will help you assess whether a nine-to-five schedule works for you or if and how to pursue an alternative arrangement. You'll learn how to make the most important people to you feel, well, important. And you'll see that making time for yourself isn't an indulgence—it's a necessity.

How to Use This Book

Because our lives are uniquely complicated and there's no single definition of success for work/life balance, there's no one way to use this book. We've selected pieces that provide research, insights, and advice from a host of experts to give you options to sample and modify as you learn what works for you—and your commitments. We've organized the content into buckets that address the areas we all find challenging: time management and decision-making, our schedules, our family—and making room for taking good care of ourselves.

We encourage you to find the sections or chapters of the book that are most appropriate for you, based on what you're currently struggling with. Jump to the section on relationships if you feel that you're always letting down people who matter to you. Flip to the section on flexible work schedules if you want to volunteer at a local animal shelter on a regular basis. If you're not quite sure where your balance is off, take the assessment in the first section to find out.

With your recommitment to your priorities as your guiding light, you can identify opportunities where there's overlap. The communication skills you hone by pitching new products at work can help you speak out on behalf of a nonprofit—to raise its visibility in the community and broaden its reach. The hard-core obstacle-course race you and your colleague sign up for can do double-duty as both a team-building and a networking exercise. (And though you'll come home with mud-soaked laundry, the experience can tick off the self-care box, too.)

Your work, self, home, and community are not separate chambers of your life that exist in isolation from each other. When you find ways to integrate the aspects of your life and the different roles you play in each, you'll be more productive and engaged in the segments of your life—and happier.

—The Editors

SECTION ONE

Take Stock

CHAPTER 1

Be a Better Leader, Have a Richer Life

by Stewart D. Friedman

IDEA IN BRIEF

Life's a zero-sum game, right? The more you strive to win in one dimension (for example, your work), the more the other three dimensions (your self, your home, and your community) must lose. Not according to Friedman. You don't have to make trade-offs among life's domains, at least, not as much as you think. Nor should you: Trading off can leave you feeling exhausted, unfulfilled, or isolated. And it hurts the people you care about most.

Reprinted from *Harvard Business Review*, April 2008 (product #R0804H).

To excel in all dimensions of life, use Friedman's **Total Leadership** process. First, articulate who and what matters most in your life. Then experiment with small changes that enhance your satisfaction and performance in *all four domains*. For example, exercising three mornings a week gives you more energy for work and improves your self-esteem and health, which makes you a better parent and friend.

Friedman's research suggests that people who focus on the concept of Total Leadership have a 14%–45% increase in satisfaction in all life domains and a 9% improvement in job performance—even while working fewer hours.

IDEA IN PRACTICE

Total Leadership helps you mitigate a range of problems that stem from making trade-offs among the different dimensions of your life:

- Feeling **unfulfilled** because you're not doing what you love
- Feeling **inauthentic** because you're not acting according to your values
- Feeling **disconnected** from people who matter to you
- Feeling **exhausted** by trying to keep up with it all

To tackle such problems using Total Leadership, take these steps:

1. **Reflect.** For each of the four domains of your life—work, home, community, and self—reflect on how important each is to you, how much time and energy you devote to each, and how satisfied you are in each. Are there discrepancies between what is important to you and how you spend your time and energy? What is your overall life satisfaction?

2. **Brainstorm possibilities.** Based on the insights you've achieved during your four-way reflection, brainstorm a long list of small experiments that may help you move closer to greater satisfaction in all four domains. These are new ways of doing things that would carry minimal risk and let you see results quickly. For example:

    - Turning off cell phones during family dinners could help you sharpen your focus on the people who matter most to you.
    - Exercising several times a week could give you more energy.
    - Joining a club with coworkers could help you forge closer friendships with them.
    - Preparing for the week ahead on Sunday evenings could help you sleep better and go into the new week refreshed.

3. **Choose experiments.** Narrow the list of experiments you've brainstormed to the three most promising. They should:

- Improve your satisfaction and performance in all four dimensions of your life.
- Have effects viewed as positive by the people who matter to you in every dimension of your life.
- Be the most costly—in regret and missed opportunities—if you *don't* do them.
- Position you to practice skills you most want to develop and do more of what you *want* to be doing.

4. **Measure progress.** Develop a scorecard for each experiment you've chosen. For example:

Exercise three mornings a week with my husband.

Domain	Goals	Measures	Actions
Work	Improving alertness and productivity	No caffeine to get through the day, better morale on my team, more productive sales calls	• Get doctor's feedback on exercise plan • Join gym • Set alarm earlier on exercise days • Tell coworkers, family, and friends about my plan, how they can help, and how it will benefit them
Home	Spending more time with husband	Fewer arguments, feeling closer	
Community	Increasing strength to participate in athletic fundraising events with friends	Three 10K fund-raising walks completed within a year	
Self	Improving self-esteem	Greater confidence	

In my research and coaching work over the past two decades, I have met many people who feel unfulfilled, overwhelmed, or stagnant because they are forsaking performance in one or more aspects of their lives. They aren't bringing their leadership abilities to bear in all of life's domains—work, home, community, and self (mind, body, and spirit). Of course, there will always be some tension among the different roles we play. But, contrary to the common wisdom, there's no reason to assume that it's a zero-sum game. It makes more sense to pursue excellent performance as a leader in all four domains—achieving what I call "four-way wins"—not trading off one for another but finding mutual value among them.

This is the main idea in a program called Total Leadership that I teach at the Wharton School and at companies and workshops around the world. "Total" because it's about the whole person and "Leadership" because it's about creating sustainable change to benefit not just you but the most important people around you.

Scoring four-way wins starts by taking a clear view of what you want from and can contribute to each domain of your life, now and in the future, with thoughtful consideration of the people who matter most to you and the expectations you have for one another. This is followed by systematically designing and implementing carefully crafted experiments—doing something new for a short period to see how it affects all four domains. If an experiment doesn't work out, you stop or adjust, and little is lost. If it does work out, it's a small win;

over time these add up so that your overall efforts are focused increasingly on what and who matters most. Either way, you learn more about how to lead in all parts of your life.

This process doesn't require inordinate risk. On the contrary, it works because it entails realistic expectations, short-term changes that are in your control, and the explicit support of those around you. Take, for instance, Kenneth Chen, a manager I met at a workshop some time ago. (All names in this article are pseudonyms.) His professional goal was to become CEO, but he had other goals as well, which on the face of it might have appeared conflicting. He had recently moved to Philadelphia and wanted to get more involved with his community. He also wished to strengthen bonds with his family. To further all of these goals, he decided to join a city-based community board, which would not only allow him to hone his leadership skills (in support of his professional goal) but also have benefits in the family domain. It would give him more in common with his sister, a teacher who gave back to the community every day, and he hoped his fiancée would participate as well, enabling them to do something together for the greater good. He would feel more spiritually alive, and this, in turn, would increase his self-confidence at work.

Now, about three years later, he reports that he is not only on a community board with his fiancée but also on the formal succession track for CEO. He's a better leader in all aspects of his life because he is acting in ways that are more consistent with his values. He is creatively enhancing his performance in all domains of his life and leading others to improve their performance by encouraging them to better integrate the different parts of their lives, too.

Kenneth is not alone. Total Leadership workshop participants assess themselves at the beginning and the end of the program, and they consistently report improvements in their effectiveness, as well as a greater sense of harmony among the once-competing domains of their lives. In a recent study over a four-month period of more than 665 business professionals (whose average age was about 35), their *satisfaction* increased by an average of 14% in their work lives, 28% in their home lives, and 31% in their community lives. Perhaps most significant, their satisfaction in the domain of the self—their physical and emotional health and their intellectual and spiritual growth—increased by 45%. But they also reported that their *performance* improved: at work (by 9%), at home (15%), in the community (12%), and personally (25%). Paradoxically, these gains were made even as participants spent less time on work and more on other aspects of their lives. They're working smarter—and they're more focused, passionate, and committed to what they're doing.

While hundreds of leaders at all levels go through this program every year, you don't need a workshop to identify worthwhile experiments (though it does help). The process is pretty straightforward, though not simple. In the sections that follow, I will give you an overview of the process and take you through the basics of designing and implementing experiments to produce four-way wins.

The Total Leadership Process

The Total Leadership concept rests on three principles:

- **Be real.** Act with authenticity by clarifying what's important.
- **Be whole.** Act with integrity by respecting the whole person.
- **Be innovative.** Act with creativity by experimenting with how things get done.

You begin the process by thinking, writing, and talking with peer coaches to identify your core values, your leadership vision, and the current alignment of your actions and values—clarifying what's important. Peer coaching is enormously valuable, at this stage and throughout, because an outside perspective provides a sounding board for your ideas, challenges you, gives you a fresh way to see the possibilities for innovation, and helps hold you accountable to your commitments.

You then identify the most important people—"key stakeholders"—in all domains and the performance expectations you have of one another. Then you talk with them: If you're like most participants, you'll be surprised to find that what, and how much, your key stakeholders actually need from you is different from, and less than, what you thought beforehand.

These insights create opportunities for you to focus your attention more intelligently, spurring innovative action. Now, with a firmer grounding in what's most important, and a more complete picture of your inner circle, you begin to see new ways of making life better, not just for you but for the people around you.

The next step is to design experiments and then try them out during a limited period of time. The best experiments are changes that your stakeholders wish for as much as, if not more than, you do.

Designing Experiments

To pursue a four-way win means to produce a change intended to fulfill multiple goals that benefit each and every domain of your life. In the domain of work, typical goals for an experiment can be captured under these broad headings: taking advantage of new opportunities for increasing productivity, reducing hidden costs, and improving the work environment. Goals for home and community tend to revolve around improving relationships and contributing more to society. For the self, it's usually about improving health and finding greater meaning in life.

As you think through the goals for your experiment, keep in mind the interests and opinions of your key stakeholders and anyone else who might be affected by the changes you are envisioning. In exploring the idea of joining a community board, for instance, Kenneth Chen sought advice from his boss, who had served on many boards, and also from the company's charitable director and the vice president of talent. In this way, he got their support. His employers could see how his participation on a board would benefit the company by developing Kenneth's leadership skills and his social network.

Some experiments benefit only a single domain directly while having indirect benefits in the others. For example, setting aside three mornings a week to exercise improves your health directly but may indirectly give you more energy for your work and raise your self-esteem, which in turn might make you a better father and friend. Other activities—such as running a half-marathon with your kids to raise funds for a charity sponsored by your company—occur in, and directly benefit, all four domains simultaneously. Whether the benefits are direct or indirect, achieving a four-way win is the goal. That's what makes the changes sustainable: Everyone benefits and wants to succeed. The expected gains need not accrue until sometime in the future, so keep in mind that some benefits may not be obvious—far-off career advancements, for instance, or a contact who might ultimately offer valuable connections.

Identify possibilities

Open your mind to what's possible and try to think of as many potential experiments as you can, describing in a sentence or two what you would do in each. This is a time to let your imagination run free. Don't worry about all the potential obstacles at this point.

At first blush, conceiving of experiments that produce benefits for all the different realms may seem a formidable task. After all, if it were easy, people wouldn't be feeling so much tension between work and the rest of their lives. But I've found that most people realize it's not that hard once they approach the challenge systematically. And, like a puzzle, it can be fun, especially if you keep in mind that experiments must fit your particular

HOW CAN I DESIGN AN EXPERIMENT TO IMPROVE ALL DOMAINS OF MY LIFE?

Our research has revealed that most successful experiments combine components of nine general categories. Thinking about possibilities in this way will make it easier for you to conceive of the small changes you can make that will mutually benefit your work, your home, your community, and yourself. Most experiments are a hybrid of some combination of these categories.

Tracking and Reflecting

Keeping a record of activities, thoughts, and feelings (and perhaps distributing it to friends, family, and coworkers) to assess progress on personal and professional goals, thereby increasing self-awareness and maintaining priorities.

Examples

- Record visits to the gym along with changes in energy levels.
- Track the times of day when you feel most engaged or most lethargic.

Planning and Organizing

Taking actions designed to better use time and prepare and plan for the future.

(*continued*)

HOW CAN I DESIGN AN EXPERIMENT TO IMPROVE ALL DOMAINS OF MY LIFE?

Examples

- Denote all activities on your calendar, not just work.
- Share your schedule with someone else.
- Prepare for the week on Sunday evening.

Rejuvenating and Restoring

Attending to body, mind, and spirit so that the tasks of daily living and working are undertaken with renewed power, focus, and commitment.

Examples

- Quit unhealthy physical habits (smoking, drinking).
- Make time for reading a novel.
- Engage in activities that improve emotional and spiritual health (yoga, meditation, etc.).

Appreciating and Caring

Having fun with people (typically, by doing things with coworkers outside work), caring for others, and appreciating relationships as a way of bonding at a basic human level to respect the whole person, which increases trust.

Examples

- Join a book group or health club with coworkers.
- Help your son complete his homework.
- Devote one day a month to community service.

Focusing and Concentrating

Being physically present, psychologically present, or both when needed to pay attention to stakeholders who matter most. Sometimes this means saying no to opportunities or obligations. Includes attempts to show more respect to important people encountered in different domains and the need to be accessible to them.

Examples

- Turn off digital communication devices at a set time.
- Set aside a specific time to focus on one thing or person.
- Review email at preset times during the day.

Revealing and Engaging

Sharing more of yourself with others—and listening—so they can better support your values and the steps

(*continued*)

HOW CAN I DESIGN AN EXPERIMENT TO IMPROVE ALL DOMAINS OF MY LIFE?

you want to take toward your leadership vision. By enhancing communication about different aspects of life, you demonstrate respect for the whole person.

Examples

- Have weekly conversations about religion with spouse.
- Describe your personal leadership vision to others.
- Mentor a new employee.

Time Shifting and "Re-Placing"

Working remotely or during different hours to increase flexibility and thus better fit in community, family, and personal activities while increasing efficiency; questioning traditional assumptions and trying new ways to get things done.

Examples

- Work from home.
- Take music lessons during your lunch hour.
- Do work during your commute.

Delegating and Developing

Reallocating tasks in ways that increase trust, free up time, and develop skills in yourself and others; working smarter by reducing or eliminating low-priority activities.

Examples

- Hire a personal assistant.
- Have a subordinate take on some of your responsibilities.

Exploring and Venturing

Taking steps toward a new job, career, or other activity that better aligns your work, home, community, and self with your core values and aspirations.

Examples

- Take on new roles at work, such as a cross-functional assignment.
- Try a new coaching style.
- Join the board of your child's day care center.

circumstances. Experiments can and do take myriad forms. But having sifted through hundreds of experiment designs, my research team and I have found that they tend to fall into nine general types. Use the nine categories described in the sidebar "How Can I Design an Experiment to Improve All Domains of My Life?" to organize your thinking.

One category of experiment involves changes in where and when work gets done. One workshop participant, a sales director for a global cement producer, tried working online from his local public library one day a week to free himself from his very long commute. This was a break from a company culture that didn't traditionally support employees working remotely, but the change benefited everyone. He had more time for outside interests, and he was more engaged and productive at work.

Another category has to do with regular self-reflection. As an example, you might keep a record of your activities, thoughts, and feelings over the course of a month to see how various actions influence your performance and quality of life. Still another category focuses on planning and organizing your time—such as trying out a new technology that coordinates commitments at work with those in the other domains.

Conversations about work and the rest of life tend to emphasize segmentation: How do I shut out the office when I am with my family? How can I eliminate distractions and concentrate purely on work? But, in some cases, it might be better to make boundaries between domains more permeable, not thicker. The very technologies that make it hard for us to maintain healthy boundaries among domains also enable us to blend them in ways—unfathomable even a decade ago—that can render us more productive and more fulfilled. These tools give us choices. The challenge we all face is learning how to use them wisely, and smart experiments give you an opportunity to increase your skill in doing so. The main point is to identify possibilities that will work well in your unique situation.

All effective experiments require that you question traditional assumptions about how things get done, as the sales director did. It's easier to feel free to do this, and to take innovative action, when you know that your goal is to improve performance in all domains and that you'll be gathering data about the impact of your experiment to determine if indeed it is working—for your key stakeholders and for you.

Whatever type you choose, the most useful experiments feel like something of a stretch: not too easy, not too daunting. It might be something quite mundane for someone else, but that doesn't matter. What's critical is that *you* see it as a moderately difficult challenge.

Choose a few, get started, and adapt

Coming up with possibilities is an exercise in unbounded imagination. But when it comes time to take action, it's not practical to try out more than three experiments at once. Typically, two turn out to be relatively successful and one goes haywire, so you will earn some small wins, and learn something useful about leadership, without biting off more than you can chew. Now the priority is to narrow the list to the three most-promising candidates by reviewing which will:

- Give you the best overall return on your investment
- Be the most costly in regret and missed opportunities if you *don't* do it
- Allow you to practice the leadership skills you most want to develop
- Be the most fun by involving more of what you want to be doing
- Move you furthest toward your vision of how you want to lead your life

Once you choose and begin to move down the road with your experiment, however, be prepared to adapt to the unforeseen. Don't become too wedded to the details of any one experiment's plan, because you will at some point be surprised and need to adjust. An executive I'll call Lim, for example, chose as one experiment to run the Chicago Marathon. He had been feeling out of shape, which in turn diminished his energy and focus both at work and at home. His wife, Joanne, was pregnant with their first child and initially supported the plan because she believed that the focus required by the training and the physical outlet it provided would make Lim a better father. The family also had a strong tradition of athleticism, and Joanne herself was an accomplished athlete. Lim was training with his boss and other colleagues, and all agreed that it would be a healthy endeavor that would improve professional communication (as they thought there would be plenty of time to bond during training).

But as her delivery date approached, Joanne became apprehensive, which she expressed to Lim as concern that he might get injured. Her real concern, though, was that he was spending so much time on an activity that might drain his energy at a point when the family needed him most. One adjustment that Lim made to reassure Joanne of his commitment to their family was to initiate another experiment in which he took the steps needed to allow him to work at home on Thursday afternoons. He had to set up some new technologies and agree to send a monthly memo to his boss summarizing what he was accomplishing on those afternoons. He also bought a baby sling, which would allow him to keep his new son with him while at home.

In the end, not only were Joanne and their baby on hand to cheer Lim on while he ran the marathon, but she ended up joining him for the second half of the race to give him a boost when she saw his energy flagging. His business unit's numbers improved during the period when he was training and working at home. So did the unit's morale—people began to see the company as more flexible, and they were encouraged to be more creative in how they got their own work done—and word got around. Executives throughout the firm began to come up with their own ideas for ways to pay more attention to other sides of their employees' lives and so build a stronger sense of community at work.

The investment in a well-designed experiment almost always pays off because you learn how to lead in new and creative ways in all parts of your life. And if your experiments turn out well—as they usually, but not always, do—it will benefit everyone: you, your business, your family, and your community.

Measuring Progress

The only way to fail with an experiment is to fail to learn from it, and this makes useful metrics essential. No doubt it's better to achieve the results you are after than to fall short, but hitting targets does not in itself advance you toward becoming the leader you want to be. Failed experiments give you, and those around you, information that helps create better ones in the future.

The sidebar "How Do I Know If My Experiment Is Working?" shows how Kenneth Chen measured his progress. He used this simple chart to spell out the intended benefits of his experiment in each of the four domains and how he would assess whether he had realized these benefits. To set up your own scorecard, use a separate sheet for each experiment; at the top of the page, write a brief description of it. Then record your goals for each domain in the first column. In the middle column, describe your results metrics: how you will measure whether the goals for each domain have been achieved. In the third column, describe your actions—the plan for the steps you will take to implement your experiment. As you begin to implement your plan, you may find that your initial indicators are too broad or too vague, so refine your scorecard as you go along to make it more useful for you. The main point is to have practical ways of measuring your outcomes and your progress toward them, and the approach you take only needs to work for you and your stakeholders.

Workshop participants have used all kinds of metrics: cost savings from reduced travel, number of email misunderstandings averted, degree of satisfaction with family time, hours spent volunteering at a teen center, and so on. Metrics may be objective or subjective, qualitative or quantitative, reported by you or by others, and frequently or intermittently observed. When it comes to frequency, for instance, it helps to consider how long you'll be able to remember what you did. For example, if you were to go on a diet to get healthier, increase energy,

HOW DO I KNOW IF MY EXPERIMENT IS WORKING?

Using this tool, an executive I'll call Kenneth Chen systematically set out in detail his various goals, the metrics he would use to measure his progress, and the steps he would take in conducting an experiment that would further those goals—joining the board of a nonprofit organization. Kenneth's worksheet is merely an example: Every person's experiments, goals, and metrics are unique.

For a more comprehensive offering of online tools, videos, podcasts and more, go to www.totalleadership.org.

(continued)

A sample scorecard

<table>
<tr><th></th><th>Experiment's goals</th><th>How I will measure success</th><th>Implementation steps</th></tr>
<tr><td>Work</td><td>• To fulfill the expectation that executives will give back to the local community
• To establish networks with other officers in my company and other professionals in the area
• To learn leadership skills from other board members and from the organization I join</td><td>• Collect business cards from everyone I meet on the board and during board meetings, and keep track of the number of professionals I meet
• After each meeting, regularly record the leadership skills of those I would like to emulate</td><td rowspan="4">☐ Meet with my manager, who has sat on many boards and can provide support and advice
☐ Meet with the director of my company's foundation to determine my real interests and to help assess what relationship our firm has with various community organizations
☐ Discuss my course of action with my fiancée and see whether joining a board interests her
☐ Sign up to attend the December 15 overview session of the Business on Board program
☐ Assess different opportunities within the community and then reach out to organizations I'm interested in
☐ Apply for membership to a community board</td></tr>
<tr><td>Home</td><td>• To join a board that can involve my fiancée, Celine
• To have something to discuss with my sister (a special education instructor)</td><td>• See whether Celine gets involved in the board
• Record the number of conversations my sister and I have about community service for the next three months and see whether they have brought us closer</td></tr>
<tr><td>Community</td><td>• To provide my leadership skills to a nonprofit organization
• To get more involved in giving back to the community</td><td>• Record what I learn about each nonprofit organization I research
• Record the number of times I attend board meetings</td></tr>
<tr><td>Self</td><td>• To feel good about contributing to others' welfare
• To see others grow as a result of my efforts
• To become more compassionate</td><td>• Assess how I feel about myself in a daily journal
• Assess the effect I have on others in terms of potential number of people affected
• Ask for feedback from others about whether I've become more compassionate</td></tr>
</table>

and enhance key relationships, food intake would be an important metric. But would you be able to remember what you ate two days ago?

Small Wins for Big Change

Experiments shouldn't be massive, all-encompassing shifts in the way you live. Highly ambitious designs usually fail because they're too much to handle. The best experiments let you try something new while minimizing the inevitable risks associated with change. When the stakes are smaller, it's easier to overcome the fear of failure that inhibits innovation. You start to see results, and others take note, which both inspires you to go further and builds support from your key stakeholders.

Another benefit of the small-wins approach to experiments is that it opens doors that would otherwise be closed. You can say to people invested in the decision, "Let's just try this. If it doesn't work, we'll go back to the old way or try something different." By framing an experiment as a trial, you reduce resistance because people are more likely to try something new if they know it's not permanent and if they have control over deciding whether the experiment is working according to *their* performance expectations.

But "small" is a relative term—what might look like a small step for you could seem like a giant leap to me, and vice versa. So don't get hung up on the word. What's more, this isn't about the scope or importance of the changes you eventually make. Large-scale change is grounded in small steps toward a big idea. So while the steps in an experiment might be small, the goals are not.

Ismail, a successful 50-year-old entrepreneur and CEO of an engineering services company, described the goal for his first experiment this way: "Restructure my company and my role in it." There's nothing small about that. He felt he was missing a sense of purpose.

Ismail designed practical steps that would allow him to move toward his large goal over time. His first experiments were small and achievable. He introduced a new method that both his colleagues and his wife could use to communicate with him. He began to hold sacrosanct time for his family and his church. As he looked for ways to free up more time, he initiated delegation experiments that had the effect of flattening his organization's structure. These small wins crossed over several domains, and eventually he did indeed transform his company and his own role in it. When I spoke with him 18 months after he'd started, he acknowledged that he'd had a hard time coping with the loss of control over tactical business matters, but he described his experiments as "a testament to the idea of winning the small battles and letting the war be won as a result." He and his leadership team both felt more confident about the firm's new organizational structure.

People try the Total Leadership program for a variety of reasons. Some feel unfulfilled because they're not doing what they love. Some don't feel genuine because they're not acting according to their values. Others feel disconnected, isolated from people who matter to them. They crave stronger relationships, built on trust, and yearn for enriched social networks. Still others are just in a rut. They want to tap into their creative energy but don't know how (and sometimes lack the courage) to do so. They feel out of control and unable to fit in all that's important to them.

My hunch is that there are more four-way wins available to you than you'd think. They are there for the taking. You have to know how to look for them and then find the support and zeal to pursue them. By providing a blueprint for how you can be real, be whole, and be innovative as a leader in all parts of your life, this program helps you perform better according to the standards of the most important people in your life; feel better in all the domains of your life; and foster greater harmony among the domains by increasing the resources available to you to fit all the parts of your life together. No matter what your career stage or current position, you can be a better leader and have a richer life—if you are ready and willing to rise to the challenge.

Stewart D. Friedman is the Professor of Management Practice Emeritus at the Wharton School. The former head of Ford Motor's Leadership Development Center, he is the author of *Leading the Life You Want: Skills for Integrating Work and Life*, *Baby Bust: New Choices for Men and Women in Work and Family*, and *Total Leadership: Be a Better Leader, Have a Richer Life*. For more, visit www.totalleadership.org, or find him on Twitter @StewFriedman or on LinkedIn.

CHAPTER 2

Assessment: Are You Focusing on What's Important to You?

by Stewart D. Friedman

In this assessment, you'll compare your priorities with how you actually allocate your time and energy.

There's an old saw that the urgent often wins over the important. But too much focus on things that aren't important to you can have significant long-term impact on your career, your family, and your health. The "Four-Way View Test," adapted from my 2008 book, *Total Leadership: Be a Better Leader, Have a Richer Life*, gives you an understanding of how you're focusing your attention on

---

Adapted from content posted on hbr.org, June 1, 2013.

the four domains of your life: work, home, community, and self. It reveals the amount of attention you pay to various aspects of your life and also asks about your satisfaction in each domain.

After taking the assessment, I'll provide you with some practical guidance on how you can start addressing some of the gaps that you may discover. If followed, this assessment can lead to plans for action that will improve your satisfaction and performance in all domains—to achieve four-way wins.

How to Do It

For the first two questions, assign a percentage to each category, but make sure the four numbers add up to 100%. (So you could have 100% in one area, but 0% in the others.) If you place as much importance or focus as much time and energy on work, career, or school as you do on the other three areas of your life combined, put "50%" in that part of the chart. If, as another example, all four domains are of equal importance to you, then put "25%" for each.

1. Consider the relative importance of each major area of your life *today*. On a percentage basis, how important is each one of the four areas to you now?

Domain	**Importance**
Work, career, or school	___%
Home, family	___%
Community, society	___%
Self: body, mind, spirit	___%
Total	100%

2. Consider how much time and energy you actually focus on each domain in a *typical* week. On a percentage basis, how much do you focus your attention on each of the four areas?

Domain	Focus of time and energy
Work, career, or school	___%
Home, family	___%
Community, society	___%
Self: body, mind, spirit	___%
Total	100%

3. How satisfied are you, currently, in each of the four areas? Indicate your satisfaction, your subjective sense of wellbeing, using a 1 to 10 scale where 1 = not at all satisfied and 10 = fully satisfied.

Domain	Not at all satisfied						Fully satisfied			
Work, career, or school	1	2	3	4	5	6	7	8	9	10
Home, family	1	2	3	4	5	6	7	8	9	10
Community, society	1	2	3	4	5	6	7	8	9	10
Self: body, mind, spirit	1	2	3	4	5	6	7	8	9	10

Diagnostic Questions

Once you've completed the assessment, look for gaps between what you say is important and what you focus on (or vice versa), and what the implications are for your level of satisfaction. Think about what your scores mean to you, and consider your responses to the following questions:

1. What are the consequences of the current choices you make about how much you focus on work, home, community, and your private self (that is, your mind, body, and spirit)?

2. What adjustments would you like to make—either in what's important or in where you focus your attention—to change any of these numbers? Specifically, what action could you take that would improve your satisfaction in all four domains?

3. What would it take to actually make these adjustments in your life?

4. How would these adjustments improve your performance and results at work, at home, in the community, and for your private self?

Getting Started on Improvements

If you see troubling gaps in your charts, don't panic. It's actually pretty common. In my experience teaching this topic at the Wharton School at the University of Pennsylvania and in companies around the world, I see that most people have opportunities to take constructive action to better connect what they care about with what they do. And by doing so they are likely to improve their satisfaction and performance in all four domains. Our research shows that this doesn't have to be a zero-sum game. The really good news is you can make big progress toward closing these gaps by starting small. One way to get started is to design a few realistic, manageable experiments, as described in chapter 1.

The most fruitful experiments help you make improvements across the four domains. At work, you may want to increase productivity or reduce hidden costs. Goals for home and community may include strengthening relationships and contributing more to social causes. For the private self, they're usually about becoming healthier and finding greater meaning in life.

How can a single experiment help you check off several—or all—of those boxes? Some experiments improve one domain directly and others indirectly. For example, being more disciplined about your diet will have a direct impact on your health, but it may also give you more energy for your work and raise your self-esteem, which in turn might make you a better parent and friend. Other activities—such as running a half-marathon with your kids to raise funds for a charity sponsored by your company—will feed all four domains simultaneously.

Whether the benefits are direct or indirect, achieving a four-way win is the goal. That's what makes the changes sustainable: Everyone gains and wants to succeed. Keep in mind that some benefits may be subtle or delayed—long-term career advancements, for instance, or a contact who might ultimately offer valuable connections.

Stewart D. Friedman is the Professor of Management Practice Emeritus at the Wharton School. The former head of Ford Motor's Leadership Development Center, he is the author of *Leading the Life You Want: Skills for Integrating Work and Life*, *Baby Bust: New Choices for Men and Women in Work and Family*, and *Total Leadership: Be a Better Leader, Have a Richer Life*. For more, visit www.totalleadership.org, or find him on Twitter @StewFriedman or on LinkedIn.

SECTION TWO

Make Decisions and Manage Your Time

CHAPTER 3

No, You Can't Have It All

by Eric C. Sinoway

Imagine that a company needs two volunteers for a high-profile, out-of-town project. Who should go? Everyone has pressures and commitments to consider. There's the young manager eager for his next promotion but worried about leaving his wife at home with their toddler and newborn son; the rising star who's already juggling long hours at work, a part-time MBA program, and the planning of her wedding; the mid-career executive who just joined a nonprofit board and doesn't want to miss his first meeting; the single colleague who would relish the assignment but is about to move her father into a

Reprinted from *Harvard Business Review*, October 2012 (product #R1210J).

nursing home; and the overweight team member with a family history of diabetes who knows the travel will cause him to blow his new diet and exercise routine.

Platitudes about the importance of work–life balance don't fully capture the complexity of those employees' situations. The pursuit of a meaningful, multifaceted life involves endless choices about both short-term tactical issues ("Should I volunteer for this project?") and long-term strategic ones ("How can I position myself to advance in my career?"). Howard Stevenson is an entrepreneur, professor, philanthropist, former chairman of Harvard Business Publishing, husband, and father who has spent four decades studying, teaching, and advising leaders in all types of organizations. He likens the challenge to walking on a balance beam while trying to juggle an egg, a crystal glass, a knife, and any number of other fragile or hazardous objects. As you progress in your career and life, more responsibilities and opportunities are tossed at you. And so at some point, to maintain your balance, you'll have to drop something. The key is to decide consciously what to relinquish instead of unwittingly letting go of the most important item.

It's hard for high-achieving people to accept that they can't have it all. Even those who recognize the limits on their time often still expect to be energetic and efficient enough to excel in every role: productive employee, inspiring boss and mentor, supportive colleague, active community member, and committed spouse, friend, parent, and child. It's a natural response to our upbringings; after all, in school we're taught that hardworking, intelligent students can get straight A's. But in the messy real world, it is impossible to do everything perfectly at the same time. You cannot pursue all your goals simultaneously or satisfy all your desires at once. And it's an emotional drain to think you can. Instead, you must focus on long-term fulfillment rather than short-term success and, at various points in your life, think carefully about your priorities.

This article presents a framework that I have developed in collaboration with Howard. It's based on his experience teaching and mentoring students and on the lessons I've learned navigating my own career and now running Axcess Worldwide. The framework is designed to help people—particularly ambitious executives—understand their limits and make the tough trade-offs that can lead to more-satisfying careers and lives.

You, the Ongoing Process

We all know that it's difficult for a company to make good strategic or tactical decisions without a mission in mind. The same holds true for individuals. Think of a jigsaw puzzle: It's much easier to put the pieces together if you look at the front of the box. But life does not come with a picture that shows what success looks like. Most of us start walking and juggling on the balance beam without thinking holistically and explicitly about what aspects of our lives we value most and how we value those things in relation to one another. Those assessments are not easy, but they are central to defining your goals and your desired legacy. It helps to carefully consider all the dimensions of your life. Howard and I have identified seven:

- Family (parents, children, siblings, in-laws, and so on)
- Social and community (friendships and community engagement)
- Spiritual (religion, philosophy, or emotional outlook)
- Physical (health and well-being)
- Material (physical environment and possessions)
- Avocational (hobbies and other nonprofessional activities)
- Career (both short- and long-term perspectives)

For each dimension, ask yourself three questions: Who do I want to be in this part of my life? How much do I want to experience this dimension? Given that I have a finite amount of time, energy, and resources, how important is this dimension relative to the others?

As you consider the answers, it's important to recognize two points. First, each dimension presents distinct challenges. It's crucial to tease them apart so that you are facing not an overwhelming whole but discrete issues that can be addressed individually. Second, your evaluation can and will change. The idea is to develop an aspirational picture of yourself for the present and a legacy vision for the future as a guide for deciding how to spend your personal resources. This is especially important when you feel you're losing your balance or are about to fumble.

Two of Howard's own life experiences offer potent examples of how to use this aspirational vision to shape decisions both large and small. The first is from the time when he was building Baupost—the money management firm he cofounded—as well as teaching at Harvard Business School. At that point, he couldn't spend as much time as he would have liked with his young children, because he was working long hours and traveling a lot. The situation reflected clear decisions he and his wife had made: He would sacrifice the family dimension of his life for a while in order to create the best long-term outcome for all of them. But Howard employed a tactical fix that honored his vision of himself as a committed husband and father. Whenever he was at home, he was fully responsive. Regardless of what else he was doing—catching up on work, reading a book, cleaning out the garage—if one of his family members asked for help with something or just wanted to talk, he would stop and engage. He knew that the emotional value from the interaction—for him and his family—would be far higher than the value of any other task. He applied clear-headed analysis to an important challenge: how to be a good father, husband, and provider while maximizing the professional dimension of his life.

Several years later, when Howard was in his late 40s and thriving at both Baupost and Harvard, he faced a much more complicated set of choices when his marriage ended. He realized he could regain his own and his sons' equilibrium only by rechanneling personal resources from his career to his family. And so he gave up his leadership role at Baupost—a job he loved, and one that might have given him an income in the tens of millions of dollars. "I needed to earn a consistently good grade as a father for an extended period," he explained. "I couldn't risk having some aspect of my family responsibilities slip through my fingers. Sure, my ego and my wallet both took big hits. But the value of having more time and energy for my kids far outweighed any incremental monetary value."

Assessing Value

Notice that in describing his experiences, Howard used the word "value." That's because he's an entrepreneur who knows that the only way to truly assess cost is to understand the value of one choice relative to another. For example, an hour spent reading to your daughter has a different value than an hour spent playing basketball with friends, and both have values different from an hour spent studying for a licensing exam or volunteering at a homeless shelter. The key is to differentiate between options that appear to be equally valuable by carefully considering how each of them advances you toward one dimension or another of your legacy vision. The following questions can help you in that process.

Where do your options fall on the needs–wants spectrum?

Needs start with food, shelter, and health; wants include diamond necklaces, round-the-world cruises, and mansions. Needs have more intrinsic value than wants. But most things fall somewhere in the middle. So the goal is to understand, in relative terms, where your options fall on the spectrum, based on your individual circumstances at a given moment and on your legacy vision. Some wants are so strong—because of habit or even peer pressure—that it's difficult to separate them from needs.

Consider two examples. (In these and the cases of Willie and Andrew, below, names and some personal details have been changed out of respect for the subjects' privacy.) The first concerns a college classmate, Carin, who gets very sad if she can't take time each day to play the piano; the hobby is so much a part of who she wants to be that it has become, in practical terms, a need, so she sacrifices in other dimensions of her life to make time for it. The second involves two former colleagues, Irwin and Bill, who work at the same firm. Both were considering buying an expensive car and a handmade Swiss watch—investments that would consume significant amounts of cash and curtail their 401(k) contributions. For Irwin, a 29-year-old trying to impress his peers, these purchases were largely wants. But for Bill, a 46-year-old who had been promoted to a senior role in the luxury division of the company and was routinely entertaining wealthy clients, the car and the watch were closer to needs: He had to present himself in a certain way to be successful.

What are the investment and opportunity costs?

Almost every decision—whether agreeing to a strategic business alliance or committing to a leadership role in a nonprofit organization—involves two kinds of costs. There's the investment cost: the time, energy, and other resources you expend. And there's the opportunity cost:

the options you forgo by investing those resources. The challenge with investment costs is to be explicit about them up front and to understand if and how incurring them will lead you to your desired, well-defined outcome.

For example, rather than blindly diving into a full-scale job search to explore new career options, which would represent a very large investment of time and energy, you can commit to spending just five hours a week for two months researching a few industries you find promising, networking with contacts who know them, and doing informational interviews with executives working in them. The goal might be to create a short list of 10 companies where you'd like to work and to pinpoint three to five roles you'd like to play at them. At the same time, be sure to weigh your opportunity costs: what you won't be able to do because you're spending five hours a week on the job search. Perhaps you'll have to stop playing in the after-work softball league or decline to participate in a new cross-division initiative at your current workplace.

Are the potential benefits worth the costs?

Expected benefits must be evaluated just as carefully as costs, and in relation to them. Does the benefit you'll receive warrant the investment you'll have to make? The songwriter Lucy Kaplansky captures this idea succinctly: "How much did it cost you? How much did you pay? And are you sorry at the end of the day?" Willie, a friend who works for a large conglomerate, was recently told by his boss that he would be well served to earn his CPA, an achievement that requires three years of coursework.

"Well served" implies a benefit, but how much of one? Would he get a promotion or a raise after earning his CPA? If so, to what level? Would he be eligible to move to other divisions in the company? If so, which ones? Willie has to answer those questions in order to decide whether the costs of this particular effort would produce acceptable returns.

Can you make a trade?

Life is full of trade-offs, but sometimes units of one element of your life can't be exchanged for units of a different element. Think of Steve Jobs, who assuredly would have paid great sums to cure his cancer. But his money could not buy him health. There was no trade to be had. Many of us face similar, albeit less consequential, challenges throughout our careers and lives as we try to exchange something we have for something else that we want. The frustration arises when the two items in question can't be traded.

Consider the case of Andrew, a managing director at a respected financial services firm. He'd spent nearly 20 years in investment banking, but thanks to the unsteady economy, the demonization of his profession, and increased regulation, he was no longer enjoying his work. He'd long dreamed of walking away from financial services and opening a small beachside restaurant, and so, at age 52, he resigned. The firm offered him a staggering sum to stay, provided he commit to a five-year contract. After a few days of consideration, Andrew agreed, but now, two years later, he's miserable and still thinking about his restaurant. He ended up exchanging freedom for wealth, and although the money seemed very big and the freedom to be gained from his new endeavor relatively small, in the end it was a bad trade.

Can you pursue your most important goals sequentially?

Howard is fond of citing a piece of advice his mother often gave him: "Remember that you may be able to have everything you want in life—just not all at once." Consciously staggering your goals may enable you to be equally successful in many dimensions over time. Mike Leven, the 74-year-old president and COO of Las Vegas Sands, has said that he decided to focus on his work dimension later than his peers, because he wanted to be a more hands-on parent when his three children were young. So he reached professional goals at 45 that many friends reached at 40; achieved wealth later than others; and secured his first really big job, as the president of Days Inn, when his kids were a bit older. He didn't slack off in the early part of his career, but he did give himself permission to pursue his top personal and professional goals—of being a great father and a successful corporate leader—at different points in his life, because he believed he couldn't achieve them simultaneously.

In today's complex, frenetic world, many of us are—like the employees described at the start of this article—struggling to chart a path toward success in our careers and a sense of fulfillment in all aspects of our lives. Any decision can be easier if you think carefully about your goals, the dimensions of yourself that are most important to you, your needs and wants, the specific costs and benefits associated with your choices, the commensurability of those choices, and whether certain goals should be sequenced instead of pursued simultaneously to give you a better chance of success. Instead of striving for work-life balance, or even worrying about juggling on the balance beam, use this framework to pursue your life's work—holistically seeking both success and satisfaction. In the real world, isn't that what "having it all" really comes down to?

Eric C. Sinoway is cofounder and president of Axcess Worldwide, a partnership development company, and the author of *Howard's Gift: Uncommon Wisdom to Inspire Your Life's Work* (St. Martin's Press, 2012).

CHAPTER 4

Make Room in Your Work Life for the Rest of Your Self

by Brianna Caza, Lakshmi Ramarajan, Erin Reid, and Stephanie Creary

Shonda Rhimes, with four television shows simultaneously in production, is an entertainment industry titan. In a recent TED talk, she described her deep passion for her work: "When I'm hard at work, when I'm deep in it, there is no other feeling . . . It is hitting every high note. It is running a marathon. It is being Beyoncé. And it is all of those things at the same time. I love working . . . A hum begins in my brain, and it grows and it grows and

Excerpted from "How to Make Room in Your Work Life for the Rest of Your Self" on hbr.org, May 30, 2018 (product #H04CW0).

that hum sounds like the open road, and I could drive it forever."

Yet, despite Rhimes's passion and unparalleled success, her deep, single-minded investment in her work drove her to the point of burnout and exhaustion. She had stopped enjoying her life. To heal, she refocused on the parts of her self—a mother, a friend, a sister, and athlete—that had been neglected because of her tunnel vision. She became more outspoken about being a woman, a mother, and an African American in the entertainment industry: "Work's hum is still a piece of me, it is just no longer all of me," she said.

Rhimes's story of overinvesting in a single facet of herself—her work identity—and then burning out is unfortunately all too common, and her story of recovering by reviving other identities is all too rare. If the hum of your career has become so deafening that you struggle to hear those other parts of your life, you're not alone. Crafting and sustaining a multifaceted identity is challenging for today's workers and their organizations. The greedy nature of our work (asking us to wear more hats, to do more, to be always on), combined with the demands of our personal lives and social pressure to be and focus on just one thing, means we need to learn how to manage our portfolio of different identities and the expectations that come with them.

Through interviews with hundreds of workers—consultants, managers, medical professionals, architects, entrepreneurs, authors, lawyers, knowledge workers, fitness professionals, educators, military officers, and journalists—we have found that the right strategies can help us harness our complex identities to benefit ourselves, our relationships, and our organizations. Our research suggests some simple changes to how you think about yourself can help you successfully manage your multiple identities and thrive as a complex and whole person.

Change How You Think About Yourself

To take command of your own story, you'll need to abandon zero-sum thinking about who you are and create and leverage connections between your identities.

Resist either/or thinking about your identities

The default tendency for many of us is to parse our "selves" into smaller, easy-to-define pieces that compete for time and attention. We think, "becoming an X takes away from my role as a Y." But identities cannot be turned on and off, even though the world sometimes seems to prefer we stay in one tidy box. As one Iranian-American woman told us: "I am not 50% Iranian and 50% American, I am 100% of both." And as biracial duchess, actress, and activist Meghan Markle once told *Elle*: "Being 'ethnically ambiguous,' as I was pegged in the industry, meant I could audition for virtually any role . . . Sadly, it didn't matter: I wasn't black enough for the black roles and I wasn't white enough for the white ones, leaving me somewhere in the middle as the ethnic chameleon who couldn't book a job."

But Markle overcame this, saying, "While my mixed heritage may have created a grey area surrounding my self-identification, keeping me with a foot on both sides of the fence, I have come to embrace that. To say who I am, to share where I'm from, to voice my pride in being a strong, confident mixed-race woman."

Don't pressure yourself into picking just one part of who you are. Having one identity does not automatically diminish another, and trying to turn identities on and off can waste time and energy. Embracing this reality can help you identify connections between your identities that you can then leverage.

Create connections between identities

Don't think about each of your identities as being independent pieces of who you are; think about how they're connected and how they might affect each other in positive ways. One approach is to use a "holistic" mindset and seek a unifying theme between your identities. For example, in one of our studies we talked to people participating in athletic events that raise money for a charitable cause (for example, a bike ride for a children's hospital in Israel). One of our participants, an observant Jew and an avid cyclist, told us: "It is the perfect confluence of all my passions—biking, giving, and Israel." Other participants described coming to view their multiple identities as a "package," in which one aspect of who they were couldn't be separated from another.

To create your own connections, ask yourself why your identities are important to you and how they relate to one another. For example, a participant in a different study explained that all of his various jobs—IT engineer, journalist, and entertainer—converged around the skill of writing. To find your unifying theme, take a step back from the day-to-day bustle of your various roles and try to find the common ground—the shared skill, meaning, or purpose of your different roles.

Another approach is to consider how your identities complement each other. For example, one person—a pastor, karate teacher, and yoga instructor—told us about reconciling her jobs into a fulfilling career. "I think Christianity doesn't really tap into the physical part of life. It does deal with the mind aspect and the spiritual aspect," she said. "My definition of a yoga teacher is just someone who helps people to develop a full spectrum practice in their life. For me, that includes the spiritual/mental/physical, body/mind/soul, the whole person." We heard similar stories from professionals in other industries about how having a variety of distinct roles allowed them to be their fuller selves.

Leverage these connections

Embracing your multiple identities can improve your ability to take others' perspectives and engage in creative and innovative behavior. Can you find ways to repurpose skills learned from one identity to another? Ask yourself: "Becoming an X allows me to be a better Y because . . . "

For example, the nurse-midwives we interviewed talked about blending their midwifery and medicalized nursing backgrounds to find innovative solutions for their patients. And a chief of radiology, charged with integrating radiology departments in two merging hospitals, found important synergies between his role identities: "From a managerial standpoint, my role is change management and navigating the hospitals through complex changes. But my clinical background and particularly experience in my area of emergency radiology has been invaluable . . . . The relationships that I developed and working with them in the ER [as a radiologist] were useful in implementing the changes that we're making here."

Connections between work and home can also be influential. We interviewed a designer who was part Mexican and part Anglo and worked on social impact projects. She described being raised in a family that was "incredibly diverse in every single way, socioeconomically, ethnically, educationally"—an experience that helped her "understand people for who they are and not any sort of label which might precede them." She brought this mindset to her work, creating a unique organizational culture at her firm that de-emphasized the role of the designer as the sole authority, and instead put decision-making power into the hands of her clients.

Change How You Relate to Others

To manage how others see and relate to us, we also need to change how we act out our identities. Sometimes relationships in one part of our lives can exert a pull that makes us ignore other aspects of who we are, or they can create challenges that make us feel like it's easier to just be unidimensional. For example, when a working father is asked by his boss to entertain visiting clients last minute, he may reluctantly agree, feeling as though he has to suppress his parental identity and commitment in order to be a good employee. Manage how others see you by finding a balance between your identities, managing your role boundaries, and establishing your authenticity.

Find your balance

You may or may not have chosen the various identities that you hold, but what you do control is how you live these identities. How you structure your time and surroundings will impact your ability to establish and maintain a sense of equilibrium. This balance will look different for everyone.

For some, this might mean devoting yourself completely to one role for a certain period of time and then later turning to your other roles to recharge. Or it can mean spending just enough time on one role to feel nourished, while mostly focusing on other roles. For instance, sometimes it may just take an hour of focused writing in the early morning for a budding entrepreneur to feel as though she is moving her side-gig forward, and then she can leave for her day job energized and inspired.

For others, balance may mean carefully planning their weeks to ensure they have dedicated time to fulfill each of their roles regularly. A management consultant told us about learning to treat his family as being as important as a client, in order to help him ensure he was able to carve out time for them during his workweek.

Manage your boundaries

Another important step is to manage boundaries in ways that protect each identity while enabling synergy between them. To do this, you need to be socially savvy and flexible. For example, some management consultants developed relationships with colleagues with whom they could be honest about their devotions to both work and family commitments. These colleagues provided emotional and practical support (such as helping them say no to additional work requests), so that they could better maintain boundaries between work and home.

Some people are increasingly using social media to control the boundaries between their identities. For example, one multiple job holder uses some outlets (Twitter, LinkedIn) for professional endeavors, and others (Facebook) for personal matters.

Present yourself authentically but thoughtfully

We all face social pressure to "be authentic." But that does not mean we have to be unfiltered and forthcoming with everything, to everyone, all of the time. We can share different aspects of who we are depending on our preferences and the circumstances.

In one of our studies, multiple jobholders slowly revealed parts of themselves when relevant to their client interactions. For instance, a childcare worker who also ran a nutrition shop only talked about her shop with parents when she felt they could benefit from some nutritional advice for their children.

Bicultural people are often adept at "code-switching," or shifting which aspect of themselves comes to the fore depending on the culture they're in. And people code-switch even within professional contexts. One Wall Street professional told us that she connects different parts of herself with different clients—she could authentically be her Southern "lite" self when she was meeting her clients in Birmingham and authentically be her New York "full-frontal self" when negotiating in Manhattan.

To be effective in today's workplace, we need to shift our mindset and actions from managing ourselves to managing our portfolio of selves. Doing so may initially increase the chaos, but once we fully embrace our complexity, we'll feel more fulfilled and contribute more to all of our identities.

Brianna Caza is an associate professor at the University of Manitoba's Asper School of Business. **Lakshmi Ramarajan** is an associate professor at Harvard Business School. **Erin Reid** is an associate professor at McMaster University's DeGroote School of Business. **Stephanie Creary** is an assistant professor at Wharton School, University of Pennsylvania.

CHAPTER 5

Before You Agree to Take on New Work, Ask Three Questions

by Regan Walsh

During the 2009 recession, I took a high-profile job with a marketing agency. On the surface, it looked like a dream opportunity. The clients were big, the pay was excellent, and given the economic climate at the time, I considered myself lucky. No, the work didn't excite me, but what would people think if I turned it down? I started on a Monday, and every morning that week I

Adapted from content posted on hbr.org, May 23, 2017 (product #H03NXM).

felt myself growing more and more uncomfortable. By Friday, while I was sitting in on a four-hour conference call in a windowless meeting room, I couldn't pretend that I wasn't miserable. I ended up quitting that day, just 4.25 days after I started and without a plan B—yet I felt instant relief.

You should take that job. You should join that board. You should take on that new client.

"Shoulds" are the things we do out of obligation because we have not thoughtfully considered our true objectives, even out of fear: What if we never get another opportunity? What will others think of us if we say no? What will we think of ourselves if we say no? Sometimes, shoulds even seem like things we *want* to do.

But, in fact, they stand in staunch opposition to our true desires, those things we hope and strive for, those opportunities that are an immediate "yes!" When we say yes to shoulds, we end up overcommitted, spread thin, and burned out. Despite our best intentions, we can end up disappointing ourselves and the people who matter most.

The truth is, achieving the best outcomes—job satisfaction, meaningful relationships, successful ventures—requires shedding our shoulds. We can do this by asking ourselves three tough questions before pursuing a path or taking on a new commitment:

What Is My Motivation?

This is about intrinsic motivators, not external ones. Intrinsic motivation is a drive that comes from within, an expression of our true desires. Extrinsic motivation is found in outside factors, such as money, prestige, or praise. It can be incredibly persuasive, to the point of pushing us to do things we wouldn't otherwise choose, but it doesn't always lead to success or happiness.

In fact, a study by Tim Judge and colleagues shows that perhaps our greatest extrinsic motivator—money—correlates with employee satisfaction only 2% of the time. On the other hand, employees who are intrinsically motivated by factors such as curiosity and fulfillment are three times more engaged than those who are extrinsically motivated, according to a study by Yoon Jik Cho and James Perry.

How do you identify your motivators? Ask yourself why you're making a specific decision. Are you considering joining that board because you feel you should say yes to such a flattering opportunity, or because you're truly passionate about the organization's mission? Are you considering that merger because you should say yes to the potential cash windfall, or because it truly aligns with your company's long-term vision? Are you considering buying tickets to that glitzy conference because you feel you should be networking, when what you really want to do is be at your daughter's soccer game?

Of course, it can be complicated to disentangle intrinsic motivations from extrinsic ones. Our motivations are not black and white. Sometimes, it might feel like you truly want to do something . . . but if you're honest, you might admit you want to do it because you want to be *seen* (by yourself and others) as a nice, generous, or smart person, rather than because you really want to do it.

If you find yourself saying yes to something solely for extrinsic rewards (praise, money, prestige), rather than intrinsic motivation (a genuine desire), stop and consider if the task is a "should" you should shed.

Does It Align with My Values?

Being able to confidently shed our shoulds comes back to aligning our decisions with our core values.

We can't do that if we don't know what those values are. It's likely that you have an idea of what you value most, but being honest with yourself and fine-tuning the reasoning behind those values will help you get better at walking away from "should" opportunities.

In their article "Do Your Commitments Match Your Convictions?" Donald Sull and Dominic Houlder suggest creating a worksheet with four columns. In the first, list the things that matter most to you, such as spending relaxed time with family or the financial security that would allow you to retire early. The authors suggest being specific (that is, not writing just "family" or "money") and listing at least five things in the first column to reflect the different facets of your life. Label the other three columns with your resources—money, time, and energy. Go through the values you listed, evaluating how much of each resource you expend on that value.

"The basic idea is to identify big gaps—stated values that receive little or none of your scarce resources or a single value that sucks a disproportionate share of money, time, and energy from other values," the authors write.

Try the values exercise, then circle back to a "should" decision you've recently made or are considering. Where does it fit into your list? Will it eat up time, money, or energy that you want to allocate to one of your other core commitments instead?

It's when values compete that this gets really hard, even for someone who coaches others on it for a living. For example, I recently agreed to a pro bono speaking engagement at a nonprofit because the cause genuinely inspired me. I also knew there was potential to make meaningful connections. As the event approached, though, I found myself feeling more and more dread, because I hadn't fully considered what I was giving up in order to speak: precious weekend time with my family.

Do I Have a Choice?

I've put this consideration last because too many of us jump to it first. We look at our calendars, see a bit of free time, and commit to something before considering whether it fits our intrinsic motivations or our values.

But, of course, it's true that sometimes we do have to do things for extrinsic reasons, or do things that take us away from our most important commitments. Every job contains some stultifying or downright unpleasant aspects. For example, people in general dislike networking, but it's part of generating new business leads.

But it is important to recognize that even things that don't feel optional often are. Self-determination theory suggests that in order to act, or to feel motivated to act, we need to feel that we're in control. We'll enjoy something more if we recognize that it's a choice.

WHAT MATTERS MOST: A WORKSHEET

by Donald Sull and Dominic Houlder

Ann Montgomery is a management consultant who has been feeling some incongruity between what she values and what she actually does day to day. She used this worksheet to take inventory of her situation. She listed her values in column one and assessed how much money, time, and energy she spends on each. The percentages listed in column two represent the portions of Ann's household income that support each of her values. The hours noted in column three represent the time Ann allocates, out of total waking hours in a week, to support her stated values. And the entries in column four denote the quality of the physical and mental energy Ann devotes to her values. Values receiving her peak attention get a "+." Values receiving her attention when she's less energetic get a "−."

Donald N. Sull is an associate professor of management practice at London Business School. **Dominic Houlder** is the associate dean of the Sloan Fellowship program at London Business School and an executive coach.

Excerpt from "Do Your Commitments Match Your Convictions?" *Harvard Business Review*, January 2005 (product #R0501H).

WHAT MATTERS MOST: A WORKSHEET

What matters to me	Money	Time	Energy
Raising healthy, balanced kids; spending mostly harmonious time with family *Time spent with kids during the week is a blur. Are we overscheduled?*	**35%** mortgage, utilities, and home maintenance **8%** trombone lessons, soccer camp, orthodontia **12%** variable expenses—bottles of merlot, food at Trader Joe's	**15 hours** "routine"—being a taxi service, cleaning up after kids, monitoring chores **5 hours** nagging and pestering kids **5 hours** "quality"—having meaningful parent-child conversations, helping with homework	−/+ − +
Doing interesting, useful work, gaining recognition *Hours are up; satisfaction isn't. Why?*		**60 hours**	+
Saving for retirement and kids' college funds; hedging against job loss	**33%**	**15 minutes** worrying about Fidelity statement **15 minutes** fantasizing about Nasdaq at 10,000	− ++
Spending time on activities that recharge my batteries (reading, writing, exercising, one-on-one time with friends, and vices I'm not going to admit to) *These always come in last. . . .*	Not much—gym fees, books, merlot, occasional dinners out, treats	**5 hours** exercising **5 hours** reading **0 hours** writing	+ − −
Maintaining close relationships—Alex (spouse), Mom, siblings, friends		**2 to 5 hours**	−/+
Contributing to the church—community service as well as money	**2%** *I'm really too busy right now*	**0 hours** on community service	
Other	**10%** (darned if I know)	**5 to 10 hours** watching TV (worse during playoffs!), drinking merlot, reading blogs and other stuff online	+

Source: Copyright © 2004 Harvard Business School Publishing Corporation. All rights reserved.

The converse is often true as well: When we feel that we *should* do something, we begin to lose our sense of autonomy. Obligation takes its place.

An attorney I work with frequently feels she should go into the office on weekends to prove her commitment to her career. The result? She is not only producing subpar work but also resenting it. She has two choices: Keep pursuing the partner track, and work those hours with a new, empowered outlook, or decide the destination is not worth the journey and step back, knowing it's the journey she wants to enjoy. Neither choice is wrong, but understanding that she owns the choice has changed her outlook.

A business executive client feels she should attend every meeting she's invited to, despite having little time for actual task completion, and then finds herself spending evening hours catching up. Does she need to be in every meeting? No. But she can make a choice: Keep going to unnecessary meetings, and live miserably, or stop attending and trust her team to do their jobs, winning back her free time.

You are the architect of your life. Don't let others design it for you. Remember that you have a choice about most shoulds.

Shedding our shoulds isn't easy. We all take on projects and commitments for the wrong reasons, because we don't think we can say no, at the expense of our values. Once you identify your shoulds, it becomes easier and easier to say no to them, and to begin saying yes to things that actually align with your goals—the things that you *really* should do.

Regan Walsh is an NYU-certified executive and life coach who focuses on helping people who are overprogrammed and underwhelmed to reclaim their lives, both personally and professionally. She is regularly asked to give keynotes and facilitate workshops on themes of work-life integration. For more information, visit www.reganwalsh.com

CHAPTER 6

Stop Work Overload by Setting These Boundaries

by Elizabeth Grace Saunders

Why is it that when your friends, your significant other, and especially your mom tell you, *You need to stop working so much!*—you hesitate? On the one hand, you know they have a point. It's unsustainable to pull 12- to 14-hour days on a consistent basis, and you feel burned out and cranky. But when it comes to setting boundaries, you stall and tell yourself and others, "It's just a busy time. It will get better soon. . . ."

Adapted from content posted on hbr.org, May 30, 2013 (product #H00AOD).

But, it doesn't. And you find yourself wedged between the fact that you can't seem to get everything done and the feeling that maybe the problem isn't the situation—it's you. You feel guilty that everyone else seems to complete everything, but you can't. You worry that if you ask for help or say, "No" to anything that everyone will discover you're an imposter who doesn't add enough value.

Although those fears are understandable, they aren't necessarily valid. As a time management coach, I've found that one of the biggest keys to achieving balance is to start objectively evaluating the fact-based aspects of your schedule, rather than letting a vague sense of fear drive your decisions. No matter how valuable a team member you may be, no one can fit 100 hours of work into 40 hours a week, or even 60 hours. You can start to make changes once you have confidence that the expectations of yourself and others really *are* unreasonable and that you can set boundaries in a respectful, constructive manner.

Here are five steps to gain that confidence, which you can apply on an individual level or a group level if you have responsibility for managing the expectations of your team:

Step 1: Develop a Time Budget

People who manage their finances well follow a few consistent principles. For one, they spend only what they have, so they avoid unnecessary debt and the corresponding stress and cost. They also make sure that they allocate their money correctly, so that they have sufficient funds for everything they need to buy. Finally, they cut costs where they can, without a significant negative impact, and make sure to put money into investments where they have a good probability of a return. The same principles apply with effective time investment. To have a clear sense of what you can reasonably handle, you should start out by calculating how many hours you have to "spend" each week. If you tend toward over-allocating time toward work, you can do the calculations in reverse. For example:

Hours per day to work = 24 − (number of hours of sleep) − (commute) − (personal commitments) − (exercise) − (self care)

By "personal commitments," I'm referring to items in your schedule that are an essential part of you feeling fulfilled. These vary from person to person but could include family time, volunteer responsibilities, social activities, or personal passions like playing the piano. Also, eating, showering, and getting ready fall under "self-care." Once you have a sense of your daily time budget, you can calculate your weekly time budget by adding up the totals for each day. For some people, each day will look similar. For others, their personal commitments create large variations in their day-to-day time budget.

Once you understand the size of your time budget, then you can evaluate the different time costs during your workday. For example, you have "maintenance" activities like answering email or planning, "execution" activities like attending meetings or completing reports, and "development" activities like networking or marketing. I recommend making a list of all the different elements of your workday and then either writing down an initial time estimate or percentage for each one. For instance, 20% of my workday consists of answering email, 50% of project work, and 30% of development activities. Make sure to not only consider the cost for a particular item but also the associated costs. For instance, a one-hour meeting could come with the related expenses of 15 minutes of travel time each way, 30 minutes of prep, and 15 minutes of follow-up. That means that the total expense comes to 2.25 hours. So if you work a nine-hour day and want to spend no more than 50% of your time in meetings, then that limits you to an average of two meetings per day and 10 meetings per week.

Step 2: Make Cuts Where You Can

After developing a time budget, you'll typically find that you really did expect more of yourself than you could possibly fit into the hours in a day. But that doesn't mean it's time to go running to your manager yet. Instead, you need to take a very careful look at how you spend your time and cut where you can, first.

One of the readers of my book took this advice to heart when she faced a major time crunch at work. Instead of trying to fight the reality of her time budget, she took this action:

> *I was (once again) up against way too many competing projects with the same deadline and then trying to juggle other ongoing and long-term projects too, which was causing lots of stress! So, I thought about what was causing the stress and tried to tackle things I had*

> *control of without just defaulting to working a lot of overtime. For example, I contacted one of the project managers with the longer-term project to see if it was possible to 'pause' my effort on his project over a two-week period, and he agreed with some negotiations. So that was about 24 hours saved over the two weeks. Then I attacked a few other aspects of the problem by recruiting some more part-time help from another department, adjusting the scope of one project, gaining an extension on another project, etc., etc. Instead of feeling overwhelmed and a victim of the circumstances, I felt SO powerful!*

You may need to take such extreme measures in times of work crisis, or you may take more subtle measures, such as taking yourself out of nonessential meetings, asking your colleagues to review items with you during one-on-one meetings instead of sending you 50 emails throughout the week, stepping off of a committee, turning off your email pop-up, or spending less time on items where spending more time to get them perfect adds little or no value. Challenge your assumptions on what you should do and how long you should spend on different activities. If possible, only commit to putting tasks on your weekly to-do list if you have space to fit them into your schedule.

Step 3: Compare Expected Versus Actual

Once you've started to come to terms with the fact that time is limited and you've taken advantage of the quick wins, you'll need to further refine your estimates to compare expected versus actual time allotments. For instance, maybe you think that email should only take one hour out of your day. But when you actually look at the time you spend, you find that it always takes two. (Any sort of tracking will do, but if you want to be precise, tools like RescueTime can help you to know exactly how you spend time on your computer.) When faced with the reality of the situation, you'll need to see if you can take time-cutting measures like writing more succinct responses, using tools like TypeIt4Me or asking for different email strategies at work. If none of those reduce the time allocation, then instead of fighting the reality, you'll need to increase your budget in that area.

Using the 80/20 rule can also help you make everything fit within your time budget. But this will require you to more fully embrace the facts that you can't do everything and you can't please everyone. For instance, as you start to look at the value from different activities, you may find that declining meetings that people would *like* you to attend, but that keep you from your highest priority tasks, is the correct answer. Or you may discover that you need to spend less time than you might have thought to make the correct amount of impact. For example, showing up for 30–45 minutes at your company happy hour may have almost as much impact as staying for two hours. By cutting out earlier, you can have time to invest an hour in exercise or finishing a proposal, which will have a dramatic return on the time investment. Although some of these choices may make people uncomfortable—especially you—the short-term discomfort caused by changing your natural default response will have a big payoff in the long term.

Step 4: Ask for Direction

If you've followed the above three steps and still can't seem to accomplish everything you need to do, it's time to take courage and ask for help. You can do so in a clear, objective way as outlined below. But before you do, bolster your confidence by looking over the facts of your time budget once more and reminding yourself that you have no reason to feel guilty or like a failure. No one can do the impossible, so the fact that you're over your time budget isn't a judgment about you, but a sign that you need to adjust your overall environment.

Here's how to approach time budget negotiations with your manager and/or people who try to put more items into your schedule:

- **Gather your facts.** Have a concise list of projects and a rough estimate of how long the various tasks take you to do. (If you've followed the above three steps, you should already have this on hand.)
- **Develop a visual.** This could look as simple as printing out your weekly calendar after having filled in both meetings and times for tasks, or as complex as displaying a full-scale project plan. The form matters less than the goal of showing the incongruence between the available time and the requested activities.
- **Present the information.** Instead of seeing this as a battle between you and the people desiring work from you, approach these expectations negotiations as strategic sessions where you are working

together to maximize the value you can contribute. Maybe a task could be demoted in priority, be delegated, or be simplified so that you can have more time to focus on the highest priority tasks. When done in this manner, asking for direction with setting priorities won't come across as disrespectful or insubordinate, but as a joint effort to work within the reality of your time limitations.

Step 5: Keep Rebalancing

Due to the dynamic nature of life and work, you can't simply set your schedule and then leave it for the next 10 years. Typically on a daily or weekly (or at the very least a monthly) basis, you will need to balance and rebalance your schedule. This means that if you had an under-allocation of time toward a particular activity one week, like processing email, you will need to spend more time on it the following week. Or maybe one week you need to completely focus on presentation prep, so the next week you catch up on meetings. The realistic goal is to have the correct allocation of time within your workweek—and between your work and nonwork time—average out correctly.

As a final word of encouragement—and warning—practicing what I've outlined will not only leave you healthier and happier, but also more humble. When you start to embrace your limits, you'll need to admit that you aren't perfect and can't do everything, especially all at once. If you have always been the go-to perfectionist on the team, this adjustment in your behavior could leave you feeling a bit at a loss in terms of your identity.

You'll need to redefine who you are such as "the person who remains calm and delivers on-time, quality work" instead of "the stressed-out team member who meets ridiculously short deadlines and never says, 'No.'" This transition will take time but will ultimately empower you to enjoy the journey and make life more pleasant for those around you too.

Elizabeth Grace Saunders is a time management coach and the founder of Real Life E Time Coaching & Speaking. She is author of *How to Invest Your Time Like Money* and *Divine Time Management*. Find out more at www.RealLifeE.com.

CHAPTER 7

Nine Practices to Help You Say No

by Peter Bregman

Irene (name and some details changed) is a great colleague. A senior manager in a large consulting firm, she pitches in when the workload gets heavy, covers for people when they're sick, and stays late when needed, which is often.

She's also a leader, serving on boards and raising money at charity auctions. She tries to be home for her kids at dinner time, but often works into the night after they've gone to sleep. That is, on nights when she's not at a business dinner.

But if you catch her in a moment of honesty, you'll find out that she doesn't feel so great. In fact, she's exhausted.

Adapted from content posted on hbr.org, February 15, 2013 (product #H00A5R).

Irene can't say no. And because she can't say no, she's spending her very limited time and already taxed energy on other people's priorities, while her own priorities fall to the wayside. I have experienced the same thing myself. So, over time, I experimented with a number of ways to strengthen my no.

Here are the nine practices I shared with Irene to help her say a strategic no in order to create space in her life for a more intentional yes.

- **Know your no.** Identify what's important to you and acknowledge what's not. If you don't know where you want to spend your time, you won't know where you don't want to spend your time. Before you can say no with confidence, you have to be clear that you want to say no. All the other steps follow this one.

- **Be appreciative.** It's almost never an insult when people make requests of you. They're asking for your help because they trust you and they believe in your capabilities to help. So thank them for thinking of you or making the request/invitation. Don't worry; this doesn't need to lead to a yes.

- **Say no to the request, not the person.** You're not rejecting the person, just declining his invitation. So make that clear. Let him know what you respect about him—maybe you admire the work he's doing, or recognize his passion or generosity. Maybe you would love to meet for lunch. Don't fake this—even if you don't like the person making the request, simply being polite and kind will communicate that you aren't rejecting him.

- **Explain why.** The particulars of your reason for saying no make very little difference. But having a reason does. Maybe you're too busy. Maybe you don't feel like what they're asking you to do plays to your strengths. Be honest about why you're saying no.
- **Be as resolute as they are pushy.** Some people don't give up easily. That's their prerogative. But without violating any of the rules above, give yourself permission to be just as pushy as they are. They'll respect you for it. You can make light of it if you want. ("I know you don't give up easily—but neither do I. I'm getting better at saying no.")
- **Practice.** Choose some easy, low-risk situations in which to practice saying no. Say no when a waiter offers you dessert. Say no when someone tries to sell you something on the street. Go into a room by yourself, shut the door, and say no out loud 10 times. It sounds crazy, but building your "no" muscle helps.
- **Establish a preemptive no.** We all have certain people in our lives who tend to make repeated, sometimes burdensome requests of us. In those cases, it's better to say no before the request even comes in. Let that person know that you're hyperfocused on a couple of things in your life and trying to reduce your obligations in all other areas.

If it's your boss who tends to make the requests, agree upfront with her about where you should be spending your time. Then, when the requests come in, you can refer to your earlier conversation.

- **Be prepared to miss out.** Some of us have a hard time saying no because we hate to miss an opportunity. And saying no always leads to a missed opportunity. But it's not just a missed opportunity; it's a tradeoff. Remind yourself that when you're saying no to the request, you are simultaneously saying yes to something you value more than the request. Both are opportunities. You're just choosing one over the other.

- **Gather your courage.** If you're someone who is used to saying yes, it will take courage to say no, especially if the person asking doesn't give up easily. You may feel like a bad friend. You might feel like you're letting someone down or not living up to expectations. Maybe you'll imagine that you'll be seen or talked about in a negative light. Those things might be the cost of reclaiming your life. You'll need courage to put up with them.

After Irene tried these practices she started working less and spending more time with her kids. She's still doing great work and she's still valued by her boss and coworkers, but they've noticed the difference too, she told me. And not all of it is positive.

They're respecting her boundaries—they don't even seem to resent her for them—but she's had to give up something she never knew was important to her: her sense of herself as someone who could do it all. It's been hard for her to feel as valued and necessary as she did when she always said yes.

"Would you rather go back to saying yes all the time?" I asked her. She answered me with a very well-practiced "No."

Peter Bregman is CEO of Bregman Partners, a company that helps successful people close their leadership gaps, grow as leaders, and inspire the people around them to get great results. Best-selling author of *18 Minutes*, his most recent book is *Leading with Emotional Courage*. He is also the host of the *Bregman Leadership Podcast*.

CHAPTER 8

Why You Need an Untouchable Day Every Week

by Neil Pasricha

I used to be one of those "wake up at 4 a.m." or "keep chugging 'til 4 a.m." guys who grinds away at work for hours while everybody else sleeps. It's how I wrote a thousand blog posts in a thousand days. But I now understand that you can only drive in the express lane for so long before the wheels come off.

I'm no longer that guy. Now when I get home after work, I soak in time with my wife and two little boys. I finally found a solution that I feel has saved my career,

---

Adapted from content posted on hbr.org, March 16, 2018 (product #H0479C).

my time, and my sanity. If you're with me right now, I bet you need this solution too: I call it "Untouchable Days."

These are days when I am literally 100% unreachable in any way . . . by anyone.

Untouchable Days have become my secret weapon to getting back on track. They're how I complete my most creative and rewarding work. To share a rough comparison, on a day when I write between meetings, I'll produce maybe 500 words a day. On an Untouchable Day, it's not unusual for me to write 5,000 words. On these days, I'm 10 times more productive.

How do I carve out Untouchable Days?

Plan Ahead

I look at my calendar *16 weeks* ahead of time, and for each week, I block out an entire day as UNTOUCHABLE. I put it in all caps just like that, too. UNTOUCHABLE. I don't write in all caps for anything else, but I allow UNTOUCHABLE days to just scream out to me.

Why 16 weeks ahead? The number of weeks isn't as important as the thinking behind it. For me, that's after my speaking schedule is locked in—but, importantly, *before anything else is*. That's a magic moment in my schedule. It's the perfect time to plant the Untouchable Day flag before anything else can claim that spot.

Cut Yourself Off

On the actual Untouchable Day itself, I picture myself sitting in a bulletproof car surrounded by two inches of thick impenetrable plastic on all sides. Nothing gets in. Nothing gets out. Meetings bounce off the windshield. Texts, alerts, and phone calls, too. My cell phone is in airplane mode all day. My laptop has Wi-Fi completely disabled. Not a single thing can bother me . . . and not a single thing does.

In Case of Emergency

But, what about emergencies, you might be wondering?

The short answer is that there really never are any. The long answer is that when my wife asked me about emergencies she didn't love my rant about how back in the day nobody had cell phones, and we were all unreachable at times. As a compromise, I told her that when I started scheduling Untouchable Days, I'd open the door of my bulletproof car for an hour at lunchtime. When I did, I came face to face with the whizzing bullets of 17 text messages, dozens of urgent-sounding emails, and endless robot-generated alerts and feeds—and precisely zero emergencies from my wife. So after a few months, we stopped doing that, and instead I just started telling her where I'd be. That gave her peace of mind that if something horrible happened, she could call the place I was working or simply drive over and find me as a last resort.

I've now pulled off Untouchable Days for a year. Nothing horrible has ever happened, and we've both grown more comfortable with zero contact throughout the day.

A Sample Untouchable Day

So what do Untouchable Days look like up close?

I think of them as having two components. There is the deep creative work. When you're in the zone, you're in a state of flow, and the big project you're working on is getting accomplished step by step by step. And then there are the nitros—little blasts of fuel you can use to prime your own pump if you hit a wall. These unproductive moments of frustration happen to all of us, and it's less important to avoid them than to simply have a mental toolkit you can whip out when they happen. What are my tools? Heading to the gym for a workout. Grabbing a pack of almonds. Getting up and simply running down the street, or going on a nature walk. After all, Thoreau said, "I believe that there is a subtle magnetism in Nature, which, if we unconsciously yield to it, will direct us aright." And Hemingway stated, "I would walk along the quais when I finished work or when I was trying to think something out. It was easier to think if I was walking and doing something or seeing people doing something that they understood." What else? A 10-minute meditation. Or switching to a new workspace. Or my wonder drug of precariously turning off airplane mode for 10 minutes (while staying off of email and text) and leaving voicemails for my parents and close friends, telling them I love them. It works every time, and I get back to work quickly because, let's be honest, nobody ever answers their phone.

Don't Delete; Reschedule

So what happens if the bulletproof car really does get bumped? Say I get an incredible speaking invite or somebody much more important than me only has *this one day* to get together? Red alert: The Untouchable Day is under threat. What do I do?

I have a simple rule. Untouchable Days may never be deleted, but they can move between the bowling-lane bumpers of the weekends. They can't jump weeks, though. They are more important than anything else I am doing, so if they need to move from a Wednesday to a Thursday or a Friday, that's fine—even if I have to move four meetings to make room. The beauty of this approach is that when you plant the Untouchable Day flag on your calendar, it really does feel permanent in your mind. You start feeling the creative high you'll get from such deep output as soon as you start booking them in.

Before I started using Untouchable Days, I treaded water—I wrote articles, I gave speeches. But something was missing. When I implemented Untouchable Days, magic happened. I wrote a new 50,000-word memoir, wrote and launched a new 60-minute keynote speech, drafted book proposals for my next three books, and completely planned and began recording my new podcast—all while traveling and giving more speeches than I ever had before.

With a year of Untouchable Days under my belt, do I *still* go through the exercise of scheduling one Untouchable Day every single week?

The honest answer is no.

Now I schedule two.

Neil Pasricha writes about living intentionally. He is the *New York Times* best-selling author of six books, including *The Book of Awesome* and *The Happiness Equation*. He hosts the award-winning podcast *3 Books*, which is a 15-year quest to uncover the world's 1,000 most formative books. He gives over 50 speeches a year at places like TED, SXSW, and Harvard University. Get his free articles at www.neil.blog.

CHAPTER 9

How to Get the Most Out of a Day Off

by Elizabeth Grace Saunders

The idea of "vacation" often conjures up thoughts of trips to faraway lands. While it's true that big trips can be fun and even refreshing, they can also take a lot of time, energy, and money. A lot of people feel exhausted just thinking about planning a vacation—not just navigating personal commitments and school breaks, but deciding how to delegate major projects or put work on hold, just so they can have a stress-free holiday. Because of this, some might put off their time away, figuring

---

Adapted from content posted on hbr.org, May 25, 2018 (product #H04CRG).

they'll get to it when their schedule isn't so demanding, only to discover at the end of the year that they haven't used up their paid time off.

In my experience as a time management coach and as a business owner, I've found that vacations don't have to be big to be significant to your health and happiness. In fact, I've been experimenting with the idea of taking "micro-vacations" on a frequent basis, usually every other week. These small bits of time off can increase my sense of happiness and the feeling of having "room to breathe."

From my point of view, micro-vacations are times off that require you to use a day or less of vacation time. Because of their shorter duration, they typically require less effort to plan. And micro-vacations usually don't require you to coordinate others taking care of your work while you're gone. Because of these benefits, micro-vacations can happen more frequently throughout the year, which allows you to recharge before you're feeling burnt out.

If you're feeling like you need a break from the day-to-day but can't find the time for an extended vacation, here are four ways to add micro-vacations to your life.

Weekend trips

Instead of limiting vacations to week-long adventures, consider a two- to three-day trip to someplace local. I'm blessed to live in Michigan, and one of my favorite weekend trips is to drive to Lake Michigan for some time in a little rented cottage on the shore or up north to a state park. Especially if you live in an urban area, traveling even a few hours can make you feel like you're in a different world.

To make the trip as refreshing as possible, consider taking time off on Friday so you can wrap up packing, get to your destination, and do a few things before calling it a night. That still leaves you with two days to explore the area. If you get home by dinnertime on Sunday, you can unpack and get the house in order before your workweek starts again.

There may be a few more emails than normal to process on Monday, but other than that, your microvacation shouldn't create any big work pileups.

Margin for personal to-do items

Sometimes getting the smallest things done can make you feel fantastic. Consider taking an afternoon—or even a full day—to take an unrushed approach to all of the nonwork tasks that you really want to do but struggle to find time to do. For example, think of those appointments like getting your hair cut, nails done, oil changed, or doctor visits. You know that you should get these taken care of but finding the time is difficult with your normal schedule.

Or perhaps you want to take the time to do items that you never seem to get to, like picking out patio furniture, unpacking the remaining boxes in the guest room, or setting up your retirement account. You technically could get these kinds of items done on a weeknight or over the weekend. But if you're consistently finding that you're not and you have the vacation time, use it to lift some of the weight from the nagging undone items list.

Shorter days for socialization

As individuals get older and particularly after they get married, there tends to be a reduction in how much time they spend with friends. One way to find time for friends without feeling like you're sacrificing your family time is to take an hour or two off in a day to meet a friend for lunch or to get together with friends before heading home. If you're allowed to split up your vacation time in these small increments, a single vacation day could easily give you four opportunities to connect with friends who you otherwise might not see at all.

If you struggle to have an uninterrupted conversation with your spouse because your kids are always around, a similar strategy can be helpful. Find days when one or both of you can take a little time off to be together. An extra hour or two will barely make a difference at work but could make a massive impact on the quality of your relationship.

Remote days for decompression

Many offices offer remote working options for some or all of the week. If that's offered and working remotely is conducive to your work style and your tasks, take advantage of that option.

Working remotely is not technically a micro-vacation, but it can often feel like one. If you have a commute of an hour or more each way, not having to commute can give you back two or more hours to your life that can be used for those personal tasks or social engagements mentioned above.

Also, for individuals who work in offices that are loud, lack windows, or where drive-by meetings are common, working remotely can be a welcome respite. Plus, you're likely to get more done. A picturesque location can also give you a new sense of calm as you approach stressful projects. I find that if I'm working in a beautiful setting, like by a lake, it almost feels as good as a vacation. My surroundings have a massive impact on how I feel.

Instead of seeing "vacation" as a large event once or twice a year, consider integrating micro-vacations into your life on a regular basis. By giving yourself permission to take time for yourself, you can increase your sense of ease with your time.

Elizabeth Grace Saunders is a time management coach and the founder of Real Life E Time Coaching & Speaking. She is author of *How to Invest Your Time Like Money* and *Divine Time Management*. Find out more at www.RealLifeE.com.

SECTION THREE

Explore Flexible Work Arrangements

CHAPTER 10

Winning Support for Flexible Work

by Amy Gallo

Many professionals seek flexible work arrangements to accommodate lives that don't mesh with a 9-to-5 day. Yet few companies have official policies or programs for alternative schedules—and just as few managers are willing or equipped to provide them for members of their teams. This doesn't mean you should give up on the idea of flextime if it would help you cut down a lengthy commute or avoid burnout. It just means that the onus is on you to propose a plan that works for you, your boss, and your company.

Adapted from content posted on hbr.org, December 1, 2010 (product #H006JJ).

What the Experts Say

Before you pursue a flexible schedule, recognize that you're likely to be bucking long-held conventions. "Traditionally, managers were reluctant to have people work remotely because of lack of trust: Are you really working, or are you eating bonbons with your friend?" explains Stewart D. Friedman, founding director of the Wharton School's Work/Life Integration Project. Even those bosses who trust their employees worry about appearing to favor certain people or allowing productivity to decline.

Still, some managers and organizations are reaping the benefits of nontraditional schedules. Research from Lotte Bailyn, MIT management professor and coauthor of *Beyond Work-Family Balance*, shows that when employees have the flexibility they need, they meet goals more easily, they're absent or tardy less often, and their morale goes up. By focusing on these upsides and thoughtfully framing your request around them, you greatly increase your chances of getting approval for an alternative work arrangement.

Define What You Want

The first step is to figure out what you're trying to accomplish. Is your goal to spend more time with family? Less time at the office? Or do you want to remove distractions so you can focus on bigger, longer-term projects? Once you're clear on your goal, decide how you can achieve it while still doing your job effectively. Options include a compressed workweek, a job share, working from home, and taking a sabbatical. Of course, not every job is suited for a flexible arrangement. Before you make a proposal, think carefully about the impact your wished-for schedule will have on your boss, your team, and your performance.

Next, investigate what policies, if any, your company has and whether there's a precedent for flexibility. You won't need to blaze a trail if one already exists.

Design It as an Experiment

Many managers will hesitate to approve a flexible schedule, especially if your organization lacks established protocols. You can allay their fears by positioning your proposal as an experiment. "Include a trial period so your boss doesn't worry that things will fall apart," says Bailyn. "He or she needs to be able to see the new way of working."

In his book *Total Leadership: Be a Better Leader, Have a Richer Life,* Friedman talks about nine types of experiments you can do to gently introduce flexibility—everything from working remotely to delegating. Whatever you propose, provide an out. Explain that if it doesn't work, you're willing to try a different arrangement or resume your former routine. "One can always go back to the original plan, but most such experiments work out very well," says Bailyn.

Ask for Team Input

"Our research has shown that flexibility only works when it's done collectively, not one-on-one between employee and employer," says Bailyn. Your team is affected by your work schedule, so you need everyone's support to make your new arrangement a success. Explain what you're trying to achieve and ask for their input. "Engage them in the planning," Bailyn says, and let your boss know that you've incorporated your colleagues' suggestions into your proposal.

Involving your team can help head off another common concern: Some bosses worry that if they grant one person flexibility, the floodgates will open and everyone will want the same arrangement. This is often an unfounded fear. Friedman points out that there's a difference between *equality* and *equity*, and, in fact, many people prefer a traditional schedule. "You don't give everyone the same thing because they don't *want* the same thing," he says.

Highlight the Benefits to the Organization

Emphasize the organizational benefits over the personal ones. "Whatever you try has to be designed very consciously to not just be about you or your family," Friedman says. "Instead, have the clear goal of improving your performance at work and making your boss successful." Demonstrate that you have considered the company's needs, that your new schedule will not be disruptive, and that it will actually have positive benefits, such as improving your productivity or increasing your relevant knowledge.

Reassess and Make Adjustments

Once your flexible schedule has been in place for three or four months, evaluate its success. Are you reaching your goals? Is the arrangement causing problems for anyone?

Because you've designed it as a trial, you'll want to report back to your boss. "Get the data to support your productivity. Show that it's working," says Friedman. And if it's not, be prepared to suggest changes.

Case Study 1: Creating a Unique Job Share

Julie Rocco was working as a program manager at Ford Motor Company when had she her first baby. She knew she wanted to return after her maternity leave, but she didn't see how she could work a 12-hour-a-day job and also be a hands-on mom. So she asked a mentor at Ford for advice. The answer? Take advantage of the company's commitment to flexible work by crafting a job that suited her. The mentor also suggested she talk to another Julie at Ford, Julie Levine, about job sharing. Levine, a mother of two, had shared a job before and wanted to try it again, not least because it would give her an opportunity to move into mainstream project development.

"It's very much like picking a spouse," Levine says of choosing the right job-share partner. "That person is your eyes and ears when you're not there." After checking each other out in what they now refer to as "a blind date," they agreed to pitch themselves as a pair to Ford's management. The plan was this: Each would work three days a week, overlapping one day—Rocco on Monday, Wednesday, and Thursday; Levine on Tuesday, Wednesday, and Friday. They opted against splitting the week in half to avoid "losing momentum" during long stretches away. Each evening, except for Wednesday, the person who'd been in the office would spend an hour and a half on the phone "downloading" the day's events to the one who'd been home. And on their days in common, they would either work together or, when things were exceptionally busy, divide and conquer. "It's our job to be seamless," they told their bosses. "We have the same outlook, the same goal, the same vision, the same work ethic. And you'll get more from us than one person could give."

"We said we would be a pilot," Levine recalls. Ford's management not only agreed, but also put the duo in charge of one of the company's highest-profile 2011 launches—the new Ford Explorer. The experiment was a success: Rocco and Levine are now known throughout the company as "the two Julies," twin dynamos. Both say the job share has made them happier at home and work, and also more effective. "One person might work a 12-hour day, go home and collapse, then have to do it all again the next day," Levine explains. "[With us], because you have to analyze your day and share it with another brain, [when] you show up the next day you're ready to run."

Case Study 2: Taking Time Off for Personal Development

Amit Desai had been working at Bayer Healthcare for 11 years when he decided he wanted to apply to Wharton's executive MBA program. However, his enrollment would mean attending a full day of school on Friday every other week and on an occasional Thursday for two years—more than 60 days away from his job as an automation project manager.

Although Bayer has official policies on telecommuting and flextime, special requests such as Desai's are decided on a case-by-case basis, so he was told to make a formal proposal. He started by looking into a similar request a previous employee had made and talking to his boss, who supported the plan with one stipulation: If a conflict ever arose, Desai would give priority to work over school. Desai agreed and created a pitch, including a detailed explanation of the MBA program and his goals in applying, a calendar of days he would be in school and how they tied into his work schedule, and a list of benefits to Bayer. "I have the ability to apply knowledge gained at school over the weekend to work on Monday," he told them. The vice president approved his request and wrote a letter endorsing his Wharton application.

Desai completed his MBA in 2011. Looking back, he says that the arrangement worked well because he was careful to coordinate with colleagues. Even though he was away from the office at set times, he reminded his immediate team when he would be out and blocked off the time in his Outlook calendar. "The stress level was low because my supervisor and peers always knew where I was," he says. And as he'd promised, he prioritized work over classes the few times that conflicts came up. He fulfilled his commitments at work while excelling in school.

Amy Gallo is a contributing editor at *Harvard Business Review* and the author of the *HBR Guide to Dealing with Conflict*. She writes and speaks about workplace dynamics. Follow her on Twitter at @amyegallo.

CHAPTER 11

Five Strategies of Successful Part-Time Work

by Vivien Corwin, Thomas B. Lawrence, and Peter J. Frost

Most professionals start working part-time to create solutions in their lives. They have young children, want to get MBAs, need to care for aging parents. All too often, though, part-time work creates as many problems as it solves. In the best-case scenario, many part-timers end up working more hours than they intended. In the worst case, they see their importance to their organizations slowly but surely fade away. Now, though, after

Reprinted from *Harvard Business Review*, July–August 2001 (product #R0107J).

two generations have wrestled with such arrangements, some part-time professionals have found strategies that are succeeding.

Notice that we say the part-time professionals themselves have found these solutions. For even though most executives would agree, at this point, that part-time work can benefit an organization, it's still up to the part-timers to do most of the heavy lifting. That's true for two reasons. The first is simple: overload. Making a part-time arrangement work takes time, energy, and creativity. Most executives, stressed already with too many day-to-day challenges to list here, see the design and maintenance of part-time work arrangements as just one more hassle. Second, most organizations give executives little in the way of guidelines or policies to help them manage part-time work. So managers have little incentive to get involved. Part-time professionals, then, are on their own in relatively uncharted territory. And, inevitably, mapmaking falls to the explorers themselves.

For the past two years, we have investigated part-time work as part of a wide-ranging research project examining issues surrounding work-life balance in the United States and Canada. We interviewed 30 part-time professionals in eight organizations, large and small, as well as 27 of their colleagues and managers. Our sample included engineers, financial analysts, information technology specialists, and consultants, among others. About 80% of the part-timers we spoke to were female, largely because so much of part-time work is driven by childcare issues, which most often affect women.

Our research revealed strong commonalities in the approaches of successful part-time professionals. Specifically they:

- Make their work-life priorities, schedules, and (if possible) plans for the future transparent to the organization;
- Broadcast the business cases for their arrangements and the nondisruptive—even positive—impact on results;
- Establish routines to protect their time at work and rituals to protect their time at home;
- Cultivate champions in senior management who not only protect them from skeptics but actively advocate for their arrangements up and down the ranks; and
- Gently but firmly remind their colleagues that, despite their part-time status, they're still in the game and cannot be ignored.

At first read, some of these strategies may sound familiar—they are, you may be thinking, the same tactics successful full-time professionals use to balance the demands of work and personal life. But look again. The means may be similar, but the end is different. Part-timers use these strategies to generate a protective environment. They're seeking to reduce resentment from full-time colleagues, which can result in marginalization. They're trying to decrease the ambiguity that may confuse their managers, colleagues, families—and sometimes even themselves. And they're aiming to make the organization more comfortable with the concept of part-time work. In the following pages, we'll take a look at these strategies in action. But first, a few words on what our research revealed about the general state of part-time professionals in business today.

The Part-Timer's Lot

Although nearly 10% of the professional labor force now works part-time, our research found that most part-time jobs are still based on informal agreements. Created on the fly by the part-timers and their bosses, these arrangements are continually adjusted to match the changing demands of work (such as a major client presentation) and home (a child's bout with the flu, say). When organizations do have formal policies about such benefits for part-timers as vacation time and sick pay, they usually serve as rough guidelines only. We found that even in the same company different part-time professionals could work under different terms concerning hours, pay, and benefits. In one department of an organization we studied, for instance, mothers returning from maternity leave were routinely granted part-time positions. In a unit two floors up, such an arrangement was unheard of. "Not even on the docket for discussion," was how one manager put it.

What's more, our research revealed, many part-time professionals feel that neither their colleagues nor the organization respects them. Many part-timers told us they took a lot of jibes about their assumed lack of commitment to work and about their "privileges," such as leaving early. And while most part-timers typically dismissed the razzing as a minor annoyance, they said some discrimination felt very real. Some, for example, were housed in their organization's "low-rent" district where, unlike other professionals, they shared office space with other part-timers. And most lost their eligibility to share in the year-end bonus pool. As one part-time financial analyst put it: "You'd really have to stand on your head, I think, to beat someone for a bonus who is full-time. 'You're part-time,' they say, 'so how could you possibly achieve beyond expectations?' But if I exceed expectations in the days that I'm here, then I should be just as eligible for a bonus as any full-timer."

Most part-timers told us they accepted the consequences of their status as part of the deal. But they also said that sometimes their confidence was eroded, and they questioned whether the arrangement was worth the effort. "Whenever someone questions my position, it sparks a thousand questions in my mind," said a director of client accounts at a worldwide public relations firm. "Am I adding as much value as everybody else? Am I learning the high-tech stuff quickly enough when I am away so often?" Such feelings of inadequacy, some part-timers revealed, can bleed into their personal lives. As the same woman added, "When I'm at work and it seems so hard to pull off a part-time job, I wonder, 'Is my daughter happy when I'm not at home?'"

Perceived discrimination, we found, makes many part-timers feel defensive about their status, which can put them on the offensive. One executive we interviewed didn't even tell her clients that she worked part-time. "I was worried they'd think I wasn't committed or wouldn't get the work done. So if a meeting came up on a Thursday or Friday, I'd be there or I'd send someone for me. I was always accessible by phone and email." Another part-timer told us she had become so defensive about her status that she took steps at work that ultimately undermined the very flexibility she sought from her part-time arrangement. If special training was offered on her day off, for instance, she'd still attend, or if a child was ill on the day of a big meeting, she'd still send him to school. When a big project was due, she'd work nights and weekends. "It's worth it," she told us, "so the organization knows I am as committed to them as they are to me." (Incidentally, this woman was not part of the group of part-time professionals from which we drew our conclusions about successful strategies.)

These stories are extreme cases. But nearly all of our respondents admitted that work regularly crept into the private areas of their lives. Study participants typically encouraged emergency calls at home, attended important meetings during their scheduled time off, and used technology to stay in touch with work. True, these practices were usually described as exceptions, but they happened often enough to suggest that the boundary between work and home is difficult to protect.

Fortunately, the picture for part-time professionals is not entirely grim—far from it. Let's take a look at the strategies that part-timers have devised to make their unique status a success.

Strategy 1: Successful part-time professionals make their work-life priorities, schedules, and (if possible) plans for the future transparent to the organization.

Although the majority of part-time professionals are women seeking more time with their children, the reasons for alternative work arrangements vary as much as the professionals themselves. Some individuals in our study worked part-time in order to go back to school; others were caring for aging parents. It's precisely because part-time professionals have such diverse motives that they need to be frank about their priorities. Such clarity paves the way for the open, honest communication on which part-time work thrives.

Would-be part-timers cannot assume their employers will automatically divine the reasons for moving to part-time status. Many bosses will shy away from knowing anything about an employee's private life in a well-intentioned effort to respect her privacy. But not knowing the part-timer's "life story," so to speak, has its consequences. A number of managers and coworkers in our study, for instance, were remarkably reluctant to contact part-timers at home. Ironically, this usually added to the part-time professionals' workloads: Once back in the office, they had to correct festering problems that could easily have been resolved through a quick call.

The most successful part-timers in our study avoided such land mines by clearly explaining to bosses and colleagues why they were working part-time, what kinds of intrusions on their home time were acceptable, and even how long they planned to stay part-time. In short, they were explicit about their priorities. One successful part-time professional, for instance, announced in writing to a wide swath of her coworkers that she was working part-time so that she could be with her young daughter in the afternoons but that she still considered her work central to her life and looked forward to returning to working full-time in 18 months. Another woman made her priorities explicit, saying she was working 20 hours a week because she had entered an eight- to 10-year time in her life when her family came first, period. These two approaches to part-time work imply two very different relationships between the part-timer and the organization. Both can succeed, however, because they are perfectly clear.

Our research showed that the more explicit employees can be about their priorities, the greater the chances are that they can sit down with their managers and shape mutually satisfying working arrangements. When part-timers clearly articulate their needs, employers can work out what degree of commitment to expect, not just at the beginning but throughout the arrangement. Consider a systems analyst for a major oil company. When he first approached his managers, he was blunt about his personal priorities: "I told them I wanted to participate more in the rearing of my children and I wanted to start my MBA. I explained that I wanted to work part-time—and, for me, that was nonnegotiable." This tough stance gave both the analyst and his management a clear understanding of what he needed as they worked together to design a feasible solution. They ended up forging an unusually favorable part-time deal for two years. The analyst would work two days a week, and the organization agreed that he would not be required to stretch his work commitments without ample notice. The analyst's project manager agreed to take up some of the slack when he, the analyst, was out of the office. The manager was prepared to step in, she explained, because the analyst had a stellar track record, and she was confident that he was making the project's success a priority.

Like the systems analyst, all the successful part-timers in our study were individuals who had formerly done outstanding full-time work. Indeed, part-time work is not a viable route for anyone who hasn't already demonstrated superiority in a traditional setting. Successful part-timers know the company ropes. They've learned the organization's rules, they've mastered those rules, and now they're ready to change them. Of course, not every part-time professional can—or wants to—set down such unequivocal terms. But making their new priorities transparent to the organization will help professionals outperform in their part-time positions just as they did when they were full-time.

Strategy 2: Successful part-time professionals broadcast the business cases for their arrangements and the nondisruptive—even positive—impact on results.

Simply put, the main reason most bosses and colleagues object to part-time work is that they suspect it will disrupt the business. They're afraid work won't get done on time or that other people, already at full capacity, will need to pick up the part-timer's unwanted assignments.

These worries are legitimate. That's why the successful part-timers in our study did not ignore or gloss over them. They addressed them head on.

First, many part-timers help their organizations to see that the arrangement makes more sense than a complete departure. This always needs to be handled with subtlety, for obvious reasons. No one likes to hear, "Consider yourself lucky you've got me at all!" But there is really no reason for being so direct. Bosses know that part-timers have successful track records—as well as insider knowledge, existing relationships, and technical expertise. They need only a slight nudge to remind them what would happen if a part-timer were to move to the competition.

Second, successful part-timers publicize the business cases for their arrangements by demonstrating that the work is still getting done, well and on time. One fundamental way they do this is by building strong alliances with their colleagues. In fact, the successful part-timers in our study involved their coworkers as much as possible in the initial transition from full-time status. One customer service engineer, for example, discussed the shift to part-time with all the members of her team before she raised the idea formally: "Politically, it would have been impossible for my boss to turn me down."

Nevertheless, a part-time arrangement will in fact change the way work gets done. In consulting businesses, for instance, with their high premium on service, the part-timer will not always be available to the client. Extra work will inevitably spill over to coworkers, causing friction among even the best-oiled groups. Therefore, successful part-timers go to great lengths to reassure colleagues that they are not simply entitled to special privileges. At times, this means reminding people that although they work less, part-timers also earn less.

At all times, it is important for part-timers to frame the extra responsibilities that fall on coworkers and subordinates as opportunities. Thus, the successful part-timer is careful to delegate work around her colleagues' development needs by, for instance, having a compatriot who needs to work on facilitation skills lead a meeting the part-timer is not going to. In this way, she can help coworkers benefit from the extra work they're given.

Finally, creating a business case for a reduced schedule often requires part-timers to redesign their work so that they, in effect, end up doing the same amount of work but more efficiently. Those part-timers we studied who were able to achieve this heightened productivity were almost always highly motivated, committed self-starters. Consider a customer service manager for a phone company. She took the job on a half-time basis. Her predecessor had held the same job full-time. The work content didn't diminish at all. In fact, it increased. But the service manager now gets the job done in half the time.

This is often the case. All the successful part-timers in our study had rich anecdotal evidence of their ability to squeeze more work into less time. And the managers interviewed in our study agreed. Said a manager of two engineers who worked part-time: "We probably get as much productivity out of our part-time professionals as we do from some of the employees who are here five days a week."

Strategy 3: Successful part-time professionals establish routines to protect their time at work and rituals to protect their time at home.

Our study showed that successful part-timers approach the pace and flow of their work in a wide variety of ways. One financial analyst at an electric utility, for instance, spread out her days in the office, working Mondays, Wednesdays, and Fridays. The benefit, she claimed, was that she stayed in touch with the work situation, and her mind was less likely to drop out of work mode. But another professional in our study—an account executive at a major oil company—stayed focused by doing just the reverse. She worked Monday through Wednesday every week.

No matter what their schedules, successful part-time professionals establish routines that are transparent to their colleagues and bosses and help them separate work and home in their own minds. From the company's perspective, we found, the nature of the routine selected is much less important than its sheer regularity. Similarly, the successful part-timers in our study demarcated home and work with personalized rituals, which again served to clarify where they were and when.

But successful part-timers don't stop at organizing their own work. They pay attention to how the work is flowing when they're not around, as well. One systems analyst, for example, described how colleagues would let work slide until Thursday because they knew she wouldn't be coming into the office until then. This led her to establish monitoring routines in which she hounded people virtually on her days off. Every day or so, she left voicemail and email messages ensuring that the flow of work continued smoothly. Communication routines let her know when she needed to put her foot down. They also let her colleagues know that she was never very far away.

Routines, of course, are easier praised than actually practiced. Business is always in flux; emergencies happen. Meetings come up unexpectedly, often throwing the airtight schedule of the part-timer into disarray. That's why in establishing their routines part-timers need to set some judicious rules about their participation in meetings.

Now it might seem logical for part-timers to attend all the meetings they can when they're in the office: After all, missing meetings on days off is already something of a political statement. It implies, "I don't care about this organization's pecking order. I come and go as I please." Few part-timers deliberately want to make such a statement. But our research suggests that a surprising number of successful part-time professionals miss meetings even on days when they are in the office, as part of their standard routine. One systems analyst we interviewed was emphatic about the need to protect her work time: "I tend to avoid meetings like the plague because they're a waste of time." In fact, successful part-timers draw on their insider knowledge of organizational routines to make tough judgment calls about which meetings they can safely ignore and which they need to attend.

Now for rituals, which are important, we found, because they fortify the boundaries between work and home that part-timers need to sustain their delicate arrangements. So one part-timer described how every week, come what may, he coaches his daughter's basketball team and attends all the games. Another part-timer who doesn't work on Fridays deliberately leaves her laptop at work on Thursday nights. Still another professional fills up her home time with piano lessons and sewing classes. "I'm not a schedule person," she said. "But I've consciously scheduled my time."

Unlike routines, rituals often have a symbolic component in that they force part-time professionals to invest not only time but also emotion into something. We heard from a number of part-timers who regularly participated in a range of community groups, from gardening clubs to dance troupes to Bible study groups. These activities demand a commitment from part-timers to people and places that are unrelated to work—and often unrelated to children and home. These rituals that part-time professionals erect in their lives are among the most effective because they genuinely break connections with the known world and forge new ties.

Strategy 4: Successful part-time professionals cultivate champions in senior management who not only protect them from skeptics but actively advocate for their arrangements up and down the ranks.

The idiosyncratic nature of part-time work makes each part-time professional an organizational innovator, with all the risks that innovation implies. And, as with any risky investment, the part-time position often requires a sponsor, someone who can influence the way the company views the shift to part-time work. Consider the experience of an IT specialist working at a gas pipeline company. She was stressed out, losing weight, and finding it impossible to do her job while raising three children. Although her coworkers were compassionate, they couldn't see how a part-time arrangement could work out without harming them. Without some senior-level support, the IT specialist wasn't going to get anywhere. But she fought hard for a change in status. She talked to a wide range of potential champions until finally she found a sympathetic ear. Although he didn't have an immediate solution, he was able to find another person looking to go part-time. Eventually, he arranged a job they could share.

All the successful part-timers in our study had champions in senior management who helped them overcome obstacles that would otherwise have caused them to fail. That was particularly true for women coming back from maternity leave who assumed (mistakenly) that there would automatically be workable part-time jobs waiting for them when they got back. Champions also play important roles after the work arrangements have been settled. Often, they run interference with clients, managers, and colleagues who may believe that part-timers aren't holding up their end of the bargain. Champions often have to intervene with clients to protect part-timers from excessive customer demands. But champions also make sure that managers are aware of part-timers' contributions and potential so that companies consider these professionals for promotions, bonuses, and choice assignments.

Finally, champions keep part-timers in the loop. They make sure that the part-timer knows what's going on behind the scenes. One champion, for instance, warned his part-time systems analyst that he hadn't been visible enough in the past couple of months: "I think you need to go and talk to your team," the champion said. "A few people are reportedly unhappy that you've been so aloof lately." Over time, a good champion accepts some responsibility for making the part-time position work, becoming the part-timer's mentor and protector.

There's no single profile of the ideal champion, but our study found them all to be highly networked change agents—individuals accustomed to using their charisma to influence people at every level of the company. They also tended to be sympathetic to the plight of part-timers because their own spouses or partners were also trying to navigate the challenges of part-time work. Their support of part-time work was, in other words, often quite personal.

Strategy 5: Successful part-time professionals gently but firmly remind their colleagues that, despite their part-time status, they're still in the game and cannot be ignored.

In addition to needing a powerful champion, the part-timer must also build a strong network of allies in the organization to avoid becoming marginalized. Unfortunately, because of their intensified work schedules, part-time professionals often focus on work to the exclusion of making small talk in the corridors. As one consultant in a public relations firm put it: "I want to stay out of politics and all the stuff that floats around. I want to focus on my job. The rest bogs me down."

Our research suggests that such behavior ultimately hurts a professional who already spends so much time away from the office. Office gossip, in particular, helps the part-timer stay tied in. In fact, staying connected turned out to be so important in our study that we've taken to defining a successful part-time professional as someone who can squander time productively at work. Consider Yvonne, the part-time financial analyst at the electric utility. She said that maintaining her social networks was one of the biggest factors in her success. "Some people say I only come in for lunch!" she said. "And I do have a lunch date almost every day that I come in. But that's how I get the informal information I need to make the part-time position work."

In addition to tuning in to gossip in these informal conversations, part-timers constantly need to emphasize what they have in common with their full-time colleagues. By saying, "I'm not so different from you," part-timers can reassure coworkers that they're not getting a special deal. Take the case of a senior auditor at the gas pipeline company, who successfully defused a coworker's envy over her attendance at a training meeting. "He came up to me and said, 'What are you doing here? Do you get paid to be trained?' 'Yes,' I gently replied. 'Every employee does.'"

The real challenge for part-timers is making their presence felt when they are so often out of the office. Interestingly, every successful part-timer in our study had some trick for staying visible in the organization despite the many hours spent away from work. Some part-timers, for example, sent voicemails on days when they weren't in the office. Some managed their own projects—and championed others' besides—to show they were very involved. One part-timer devised an elaborate series of meetings, planned and announced long in advance. "Just in case anyone has any doubts," she said defiantly. "I'm around and intend to be for a long time." Successful part-timers show that they cannot be ignored.

Begun more than 20 years ago, part-time professional work is an experiment that has met with mixed results. In most cases, the arrangement is an attempt to give a woman more time to raise her family. But it is not necessarily a panacea for striking a balance between work and life. Many part-timers are forced to work longer hours than they contracted for, and many suffer under the second-class status of part-time work.

At the same time, part-time work makes organizations uncomfortable. It raises obvious questions about who will pick up the slack. And it raises more fundamental questions about the very nature of professional work itself. What exactly is a professional being paid for? Time or output? When limits are placed on time and pay, how should that fairly be reflected in the work?

Successful part-timers face such difficulties head on. The five strategies we've distilled from the experience of the successful part-timers work together to overcome these challenges. They not only help the part-timer deal with the organization but also make the organization itself more receptive to the possibilities of part-time work.

Vivien Corwin is the academic director of the Master of Management program and an assistant teaching professor at the University of Victoria's Peter B. Gustavson School of Business. She also works as a strategic advisor and facilitator for a number of corporate clients, with a particular focus on topics such as strategy development, employee engagement, organizational culture, collaboration, and leading change. **Thomas B. Lawrence** is an associate professor at the University of Victoria's Faculty of Business. **Peter J. Frost** was the Edgar F. Kaiser Professor of Organizational Behavior at the University of British Columbia's Faculty of Commerce and Business Administration in Vancouver.

CHAPTER 12

Staying Focused When You're Working from Home

by Elizabeth Grace Saunders

No commute. No drive-by meetings. No dress code. Remote working can seem like a dream—until personal obligations get in the way. These distractions are easy to ignore in an office, but at home it can be difficult to draw the line between personal and professional time.

Consider when you're working on a project and get a call from a friend. You know you need to finish your

Adapted from "How to Stay Focused When You're Working from Home" on hbr.org, September 28, 2017 (product #H03WZ4).

work, but you feel rude for not talking when you *technically* could. Or think about when you're planning your daily to-do list, but also need to decide when you'll squeeze in your personal commitments. Taking the time to put a few loads of laundry in the washer midday can seem like a quick task—until you find yourself making up that work time late at night. In the end, it's never entirely clear when you're really "on" or "off."

As someone who has worked from home for 12 years, and been a time management coach for remote workers, I've seen and experienced the good, the bad, and the ugly. I've found that the most focused and effective remote workers set up boundaries for themselves so that they can actually get work done.

Here are some tips for how you can make remote work more productive and satisfying, whether it's an everyday occurrence or an occasional day away from the office.

Establish Working Hours

It may sound silly, but if you want to have a focused day of work, pretend you're not working from home. Before I became a time management coach, my schedule was chaotic. I didn't have a set time that I would be at my computer, and I would often schedule personal appointments or run errands during the day. And since my personal life didn't have boundaries, my work life didn't either. When I was home, I would feel guilty for not checking business email at all hours of the day and night. I never felt that I could truly rest.

But a big shift occurred when I set up "office hours" for working from home (for me, that was about 9 a.m. to

6 p.m. most weekdays) and clarified what was or wasn't acceptable to do during that time. I'd ask myself, "If I was in an office, would I do this task during the day?" If the answer was no, I knew I needed to do the activity before or after office hours. Household chores, errands, and spending time with friends all became activities that needed to happen before or after work. Sure, I would still field an occasional call from a friend during my lunch break, or if I had an urgent task like an emergency car repair, I'd make it happen during the day. But these were exceptions, not the rule. In setting this boundary, I not only created dedicated work time but also found that I could focus on personal items guilt-free "after hours."

Structure Your Day for Success

Maximize the effectiveness of your time at home by structuring it differently than a typical workday. For example, if you work from home just one day a week or only occasionally, make it a meeting-free day. If you can't entirely avoid meetings, reserve at least half a day for focused work. Choose a time that works best for you, based on any required meetings and your energy levels.

Then define one to two key assignments that you want to accomplish during this time. These could be tasks that require an hour or more of uninterrupted attention, or they could be items that simply require more creative, strategic thinking than you may be able to achieve in the office environment. It's also helpful to shut down your email during this period—or at least stay away from it for an hour at a time. Alert any colleagues of times that you'll be disconnected, so they won't be surprised by a delayed response.

Set Boundaries with Others

To make your efforts stick, be clear with the people who might see your work-at-home days as simply days you're at home. Explain to friends, family, and other acquaintances that the days you're working remotely aren't opportunities for nonwork-related activities. For example, if you're home with your spouse, tell him or her, "I'm planning on being on my computer from 8 a.m. to 5 p.m. today. I'm happy to chat at lunch, but other than that I'll be occupied." Typically, when you set expectations and stick to them (say, really stopping at 5 p.m.), people understand your limits instead of assuming you'll be available. (I also recommend having a place where you're physically separated from anyone else who might be home, such as an office or bedroom where you can shut the door and be out of sight.)

In situations where you may have unexpected visitors, you'll need to be diplomatic. If a neighbor pops by, be open for a conversation for a few minutes, just as you would with a colleague who stops by your desk. But don't suggest they come in for a cup of coffee or have an extended discussion. Instead, use a graceful exit line like "It was so wonderful to talk with you, but I've got some work to finish up," and then set a time to meet up after hours or on a weekend. Or, if your landlord says he'd like to stop by to do some repairs, offer a time or day that works best for you, rather than letting him take the lead.

If you do need to take on nonwork-related requests during the day, set expectations for how much time you have, based on what your schedule is like in the office. For example, if your family asks you to run errands, estimate what you can do during a lunch hour, then commit only to that. For example, say, "I'm happy to pick up the dry cleaning and some milk at lunch, but I won't have time for full-scale grocery shopping until after work." Or break down errands into smaller pieces, such as, "I can drop off the car at the mechanic today but won't get to calling about the health insurance question until tomorrow."

When you explain your limits, you don't need to apologize. Lay them out in a matter-of-fact fashion, showing the same respect for your time working from home that you would have if you were on-site. As you consistently communicate and live by these expectations, other people will begin to expect them, and you'll find yourself having more time for focused work.

Elizabeth Grace Saunders is a time management coach and the founder of Real Life E Time Coaching & Speaking. She is author of *How to Invest Your Time Like Money* and *Divine Time Management*. Find out more at www.RealLifeE.com.

CHAPTER 13

What to Do When a Personal Crisis Is Hurting Your Professional Life

by Amy Gallo

At some point, we all confront a stressful life event or personal crisis that threatens to distract us from work. Perhaps it's tending to a sick family member, coping with your own illness, or dealing with a divorce. These are all incredibly tough situations to navigate personally—let alone professionally. Should you disclose what's happening to your manager and colleagues? How do you ask for

Adapted from content posted on hbr.org, November 16, 2017 (product #H040YH).

what you need, such as flexible hours or a reduced workload? And how do you know if you should take a leave of absence?

What the Experts Say

"This is life, and these things happen to everybody," says Anne Kreamer, author of *It's Always Personal.* But knowing you're in good company is not necessarily a comfort, especially if you're struggling to stay on top of your responsibilities at home and work. If you've reached the point where you say to yourself, "I can't get my job done," it may be time to ask for help, says Jane Dutton, a professor at the University of Michigan's Ross School of Business and coauthor of *Awakening Compassion at Work.* Here's some advice on how to navigate work when you're having a personal crisis.

Decide What You Need

First, take stock of the resources you have at hand "both inside and outside the organization" to help you through this crisis, Dutton says. Are there friends or family who might be able to pitch in? Do you have team members who might be able to cover some of your responsibilities in the short term? What you need may not be huge. "It might be as simple as leaving work early on Fridays for a month," Dutton says. The key is to figure out what will help ease the pressure.

Consider How Important Privacy Is to You

Before you ask for help, however, consider how much you're comfortable sharing. "This has to be an individual choice," Kreamer says. "There are many different reasons why people choose to maintain their privacy," especially about illnesses that carry a stigma. Uncertainty about your standing in the organization is another reason to be reserved, she adds. Dutton agrees, noting that, in some cases, "it can be dangerous to disclose your situation." She suggests assessing the risks with questions like: What kind of culture am I in? Are there formal procedures for handling this? Do I need to go to HR? Are there people in my unit who can be helpful? Are my coworkers going to treat me humanely, or do I need to think about how to protect myself?

It's Better to Share If You Feel OK Doing So

If you do feel that it's safe to share, it's often better to do so. "We've been encouraged to keep the boundaries between private and professional distinct, but that's not always helpful," Kreamer says. In fact, research by Ashley Hardin, a professor at Washington University's Olin Business School, shows that when you allow coworkers to discover more about your personal life, they are more motivated to meet your needs. "If the situation is interfering with your ability to complete your job, it's likely that your coworkers may already realize something is amiss, and in that case you are better off letting them in on what is going on," Hardin explains. You can also give permission to your close colleagues to share your circumstances with other coworkers if it is too difficult for you to tell them directly. "This type of indirect disclosure can open up a space for your teammates to brainstorm ways to help you," Hardin adds.

Set Boundaries

This doesn't mean you need to sit down with everyone and explain your situation in agonizing detail. Set boundaries for yourself and for others. You can turn to close colleagues for the more personal conversations, but keep in mind that "most people don't want to know every detail of your parent's chemotherapy. They want to know the pertinent information and how it's going to affect them," Kreamer says. Also, it can be tough to answer lots of questions and rehash the details of a sad situation, so don't be afraid to redirect the conversation back to work if a coworker continually inquires about the details. You might say: "Right now, it helps my sanity to stay focused on work. Is it OK with you if we talk about the project instead?"

Ask for Specific Help

"Ideally, when you share the news, your colleagues will say: 'I'm going to do such-and-such for you. Are you cool with that?'" Kreamer says. But if your coworkers aren't forthcoming about offering help, ask for it explicitly. And be thoughtful about how you frame your request. Research by Wayne Baker, a professor at the Ross School of Business, shows that how you frame your appeal strongly influences whether someone will agree to it. He recommends making the request specific and describing why the help is meaningful to you: We "often assume that the importance of a request is obvious, but it rarely is." And as with any request you make at work, give a deadline. So you might say, "I'd love your help over the next two weeks while I'm out caring for my mother. Would you be able to complete the report we've been working on? It would free up my mind to focus on what I need to do at home."

Approach Your Boss

It's also a good idea to loop your boss into what's happening, assuming you feel comfortable doing so. If you have a very close relationship, tell them first and brainstorm ideas for reducing or covering your workload. But, in most cases, Kreamer says, it's best to talk to your manager when you already "have some notion of how you intend to handle the problem." Run a tentative plan by your manager, outlining the time period you expect to be absent or working less, the colleagues who might step up for you, and whether you've already discussed that possibility with them. Then ask for your boss's input.

Do What's Right for You

There is no right answer when handling a crisis situation. Some people might find comfort in coming in to work every day. Kreamer did that when she was dealing with three family deaths—her parents and a grandmother—within six months. "I was overwhelmed by the tsunami of death, and work was very much a solace for me," she says. "Work is often an antidote, a space where you can forget about what's happening and operate as a functioning adult rather than feeling helpless in the face of these events." For others, it might be better to take an official leave of absence. "When you believe that you won't be able to function at the caliber that your job requires of you, it may be better to remove yourself from that situation for a time to recharge your batteries," Kreamer says. "When you push forward and don't allow yourself to feel the grief, you don't recover as quickly." Facebook is leading the way in offering generous bereavement leave, in the wake of COO Sheryl Sandberg's losing her husband, but not all companies offer paid leave, so there are financial and career implications to consider. Still, even a short leave—just a few weeks—might be enough time.

Case Study: Ask for What You Need

The day that Jisella Dolan received a job offer from Home Instead, an in-home care organization for the elderly, she learned that her father had six to 18 months to live. Looking at the company's vacation policies, and thinking of how often she would have to travel to her parents' town, eight hours away, she didn't know how she could make it work.

Because she didn't know her prospective boss very well, Jisella was hesitant to share her situation with him. "He was basically a stranger to me. I had no sense of how he would respond to my story," she explains.

She assumed that Home Instead wouldn't allow extra time and "didn't want to ask for special favors, especially as a new employee." But it was her "dream job," so she decided to explain the situation. "I had to be honest about how it might impact my ability" to do the job, she says. She was clear that she would need to leave work early on Fridays to travel to see her parents and probably take calls from her mother during her workday.

Jisella's soon-to-be boss surprised her. "They acknowledged and honored the position I was in and shared that they would work with me" on a solution. She was still expected to work hard. But, even when an emergency with her dad forced her to leave an important meeting, no one questioned it.

The experience "bred instant loyalty to the organization," she adds. Their "willingness to accommodate my needs made me more passionate about doing good work for them."

Jisella's father passed away six months after she accepted her job. Ten years later, she is still at Home Instead and now serves as its chief advocacy officer.

Amy Gallo is a contributing editor at *Harvard Business Review* and the author of the *HBR Guide to Dealing with Conflict*. She writes and speaks about workplace dynamics. Follow her on Twitter at @amyegallo.

SECTION FOUR

Manage Your Relationships

CHAPTER 14

Being Too Busy for Friends Won't Help Your Career

by Neal J. Roese

Friendship matters.

Everything we do to succeed in our careers is improved when we're supported by a foundation of strong, stable friendships. Basic research tells us this is so, yet many who focus on their careers run the risk of losing touch with their closest social connections.

Psychologists define close friends as those nonrelatives whose birthdays we celebrate, with whom we discuss intimate matters such as work or marital stress,

---

Adapted from content posted on hbr.org, July 28, 2017 (product #H03TA5).

and whom we might call upon for help with a move or a medical emergency.

These people are critical for both our psychological and physical well-being. The number and strength of our friendships has long been a consistent predictor of emotional well-being. And beyond the psychological benefits, friendships can influence our basic physiology, as shown by studies that link social connections to cellular-level protection against disease. We are less likely to catch a cold or suffer from acute stress responses if we have a solid network of friends. In a recent meta-analysis of 148 studies, having strong social relationships was associated with a 50% reduction in risk of mortality.

But maintaining close friendships is increasingly a challenge for ambitious professionals. The problem becomes all too clear when you look at how regretful people tend to feel about losing touch with friends.

Regret and Relationships

Psychological research has examined what adults tend to regret later in life, and there is a clear pattern of top regrets centering on love and work—that is, romantic, family, and friend relationships on the one hand and career, work, and education on the other hand. (Regrets about financial missteps rank just below these love and work regrets.) My research with Mike Morrison and Kai Epstude, for example, surveyed over 1,300 people across five studies and found that people's largest regrets revolved around relationships and career. People described their regrets about relationships much more intensely than those about careers and other nonsocial aspects of their lives. What concerned them most was the absence, dysfunction, or loss of social connections. Further, we found that the intensity of social regret was related to how much people felt their fundamental *need to belong* was threatened by the lack or loss of relationships. Romantic relationships ranked first in frequency of regrets, followed closely by family relationships—and friendships were eighth. What this tells us is that many people can recognize the immediate importance of putting time into romantic and family relationships, but friendships are not quite so top of mind. Friendships can easily be neglected.

The Challenge of Friendship Today

Part of the challenge today is that our definition of friendship keeps changing. We're developing larger social networks but ending up with weaker intimate ties. Despite being overcommitted to work and family obligations, having unprecedented geographic mobility, telecommuting instead of working beside colleagues, and tapping or tweeting instead of talking, we seem to have a lot of friends: about 200 social media friends and 11 offline friends. But in terms of close friendships, we average only about five, and for the most intimate friends, with whom we would share, for example, details on our sex lives, we average around two (down from about three in 1985). We can expect busier schedules and career demands to only make it more challenging to build, prioritize, and maintain intimate friendships.

Steps Toward More Meaningful Friendships

Friendships have never been more important for effective career performance. Research has shown that friends make you better on the job and help you earn more, partly because they provide an emotional buffer that keeps you motivated and focused. So it's important to think about how you can improve the depth, value, and longevity of your friendships.

Make the effort

People regret losing connections to once-close friends but may be less likely to notice the importance of friendships, as compared with romantic and family connections. If you're early in your career, now is the time to make the extra effort to develop and maintain your friendships. This means counteracting the natural drift away from friends that most of us experience, especially after our 20s, as we focus more intently on careers and starting a family. Call a close friend instead of just clicking on their Facebook page; make plans rather than excuses. Face time (and I don't mean the iPhone version) trumps Facebook time. Men struggle more than women with maintaining one-on-one relationships, so they may have to work harder to get time with friends onto the calendar.

Ask for your friends' perspectives

Having friends is important, but so is how we interact with them. Close friends are especially helpful at right-ing our distorted perceptions of ourselves, whether with regard to a promotion we didn't win or a romantic relationship gone sour. Friends help us celebrate our wins with more vigor and move on from losses with heads held higher. The very act of sharing and connecting can help strengthen and preserve close friendships.

Plan around shared interests

Get small groups together with a particular theme in mind, like seeing a movie, trying a new kind of cuisine, organizing for a political event, or addressing a particular career issue.

Make new friends

A challenge in today's global economy is moving to a new city or country and leaving behind an established friend network. What does a New Yorker do upon arriving in Singapore for a one-year assignment? It has been so easy to connect with others online who share our same passions. Seek out like-minded people who live nearby and meet up face to face.

Prioritize work and friendships

Progressing at work and maintaining friendships may seem mutually exclusive, given the time and effort that both involve, but they're not. Go ahead and set ambitious career goals, but don't sacrifice close ties in the process; give each one the energy required. Career and friendships can reinforce each other, as when friends at different firms get together to share big-picture career insights, inspiring each person's passion for professional growth.

Research shows that friendship matters, yet the challenges to maintaining strong, intimate social connections have never been more severe. There is no special magic to making and keeping friends. At the end of the day, strengthening friendships is as difficult as managing a career, but by taking the above steps, and most of all by recognizing that friendships demand prioritization and effort, you can boost your career performance and your life satisfaction at the same time.

Neal J. Roese is the S. C. Johnson Chair in Global Marketing at the Kellogg School of Management at Northwestern University.

CHAPTER 15

Two-Career Couples Need Long-Term Plans

by Avivah Wittenberg-Cox

"We learned to take the long view, mostly because we didn't have any other choice," says Kate, now in her 60s and busy investing in the next generation of entrepreneurs. "Both sticking to our full-time corporate jobs or one of us becoming a full-time parent weren't attractive options to us. We wanted to change the model, not just flip it."

Kate and her husband, Matthew, were a classic dual-career couple. They met in business school, married, and

---

Adapted from "Being a Two-Career Couple Requires a Long-Term Plan" on hbr.org, February 26, 2018 (product #H046QX).

settled into two demanding corporate jobs. But Kate quickly saw that there were too many layers to get to the top anytime soon in her firm. Matthew had a quicker route in his flatter organization. When the couple decided to have children, they sat down and strategized together. How could they design two careers that could give them both what they wanted: meaningful work, financial security, and a great family?

One of their innovations was to plan a lifetime family career—together. Most of us want to support our partners and their careers. But thinking about two careers individually and then trying to marry them together is often a design challenge. Matthew and Kate started with designing a life, and retrofitted to identify careers that might deliver it. They devised a single vision for themselves as a couple—and the family they had just started. They thought of it as a team vision, like they might at work. What were their respective strengths and dreams? How could they use each other to guarantee the success of their broader vision, while minimizing some of the risks they might bump into along their road? It wasn't so much the plan that helped them, they found. It was the conversation and the search for complementarity. They were each agreeing to contribute to building something that fit them both, over a lifespan.

In their 30s, they decided that Kate would leave her corporate job to gain the flexibility she prioritized short-term to care for their two young children. Matthew would continue in his corporate role to cover this life phase's financial needs. She would launch a business she had identified as having serious potential, and test run it. If it worked, he could join her later down the road to scale and sell it, and they would be able to reinvent themselves again.

And it worked.

From the Sum of Two to the Power of Two

Dual-income couples are now the norm: over two-thirds of couples in Canada and the United Kingdom, and 60% of couples in the United States. They are beginning to realize they may each be the other's most significant career asset.

Not only can your working spouse mitigate risks like being made redundant, they can also serve as a trampoline to allow you a shot at your dream, whether it's a novel or a nonprofit, a startup, or a soap opera, and whether you grab it in your 30s or your 60s.

This is a whole new, potentially delightful, ballgame. It wasn't possible in an earlier era of single-earner families, where the financial burden historically (and often still psychically) fell to the man. Nor is it true today in the growing number of couples who simply flip the gender roles but still stick to the same model. (Nor among single-parent households, dominated by women.) These options have little flexibility, and less security, in increasingly volatile economic times.

But for too many dual-career couples, even in an era of supposed equality, two individuals can end up competing for short-term trade-offs rather than cooperating for longer-term, mutually beneficial gains. Couples end up negotiating based on current realities rather than pacing themselves for the long (and lengthening) haul. This translates into decisions made according to who has the higher income, the assignment abroad, or the babies. How many couples decide that one parent will stay home, because the cost of childcare is more than one parent's (still usually mom's) income? They forget to calculate the impact of that choice on that parent's career, on their lifetime earning potential (opting out can cost up to $1 million in lost income), and on the couple's opportunities to switch roles or combine them.

As careers morph into 50-year marathons rather than 30-year sprints, we may also want to think of couple careers over much longer time frames. We still let too many decisions made in our 30s seal our professional fate for decades. How much more reassuring to know that you can hand the baton back and forth—and still finish the race in style. We may find that primary caregivers increasingly become later-life entrepreneurs when their children are grown. And that corporate titans are delighted to retire into honorary bag carriers for their newly jet-setting spouses.

Flex Your Mind to Find Your Model

For many, there is more focus on innovation at work than at home. So invite a little brainstorming into your family boardroom (the dinner table). What's your model? Are you both happy with your respective roles as currently defined? Is there a dream one or both of you feel it's time to dust off and discuss?

Here are some of the models I've seen couples define, negotiate, and enjoy, sometimes only for a phase, sometimes for a lifetime. All of them work, as long as both halves are aligned and agreed—at least for the moment.

Single Career

A historic classic: One partner has the career that defines everything else. The spouse and children follow that career. This often allows for high salaries, and gives one partner total work focus. The other partner is open to all other roles, without having to worry about income. But the couple is more at risk of unexpected and complete loss of income. The nonworking partner will find it much harder to recover from eventual separations or divorce and will often not be putting anything aside for pensions. One of the challenges for many senior women (most of whom have working partners) is that they sit on senior teams dominated by men with nonworking wives. This puts them at a competitive disadvantage when the team cultures created by single-career spouses lean toward the 24/7. Because they can.

Lead Career

A version of the single career, where one career is clearly dominant and will define where the couple lives and where they might move to. The other partner has a part-time or flexible freelance, teaching, or online career. This sports the same advantages, and some mitigation of the disadvantages of, the single-career model. For example, Jo followed her oil executive partner around the globe and turned her trailing-spouse role into a profession. She wrote books about how to reinvent yourself and became an online editor and writer's coach.

Alternators

Many couples opt for this model, which they see as an egalitarian alternation of opportunity. Each has first dibs for the next promotion or geographic move, and the other agrees to adjust in function. This doesn't always mean the other partner follows, with family in tow. Sometimes families stay in one place, and the roving partner commutes a lot. In multinational companies, surprising numbers of spouses live apart, sometimes for years. This approach can get a little bit transactional if it is held to too inflexibly. When "my turn" becomes absolute, couples lose the balance they were aiming to build. Helen and her husband Rob, a highly successful and very visible pair of CEOs, alternated weeks throughout the year. Each would be able to fully focus on work, travel, and urgencies one week out of two. The other week, they'd have primary responsibility for everything else. It allowed them to be able to enjoy both roles fully and regularly.

Parallelograms

This model involves two parallel, high-powered careers in what is sometimes called a "power couple." Increasing in number, these careers are often mutually reinforcing, with professional networks and knowledge that feed each other, think *House of Cards*. These couples love to talk shop and share what's going on in their careers, because it will nourish the other. These couples can learn from each other, buy from each other's companies. Juliet and Andrew run two separate but related businesses, in which one heads the for-profit arm and the other the nonprofit arm. Together, they make a successful combination. The risk here is usually for the family. Children may not get quite as much attention as they'd like; their parents are too excited talking to each other. Two big careers are particularly frustrating to employers these days, as these couples are increasingly less mobile geographically. The seniority of the other partner's job is not always easy to replicate or transfer.

Complements

Diversity in couple careers can be as beneficial as diversity in any team. Couples with very different kinds of careers, with different phases, peak periods, and time frames often find life a bit easier to sort out. Pressure points are often not at the same time of the year or at the same phase of life, so that they can be more easily managed. This covers a vast range of occupations, from the corporate career and the academic, to the entrepreneur and the writer. George and Anne used day and night shifts as their differentiator, with one being a nurse at night, the other an engineer by day. They overlapped for breakfast and dinner . . . Juliet was a flexible freelancer when her children were young; her husband, John, loved his corporate work in social responsibility. When the children were older, her business took off. John retired early from an illustrious career and was able to travel the globe with his now big-earning wife and her successful business. Another advantage of very different tracks is it takes away some of the competition between careers that can overlap if they are similar. Having two lawyers or two consultants who progress at disparate speeds in one marriage, especially if there are childcare choices involved, can lead to conflict. Different careers tend to have varying success criteria and life cycles, which can work together well.

Whatever the model, the secret lies in the co-design. You may move from one model to another over the course of ever-longer careers, and that may even be part of the plan. But it helps to be able to put a name on what you're both doing and acknowledge the advantages and risks of each option at different phases of life. Family careers offer flexibility, security, and options. Two people end up with a supportive partner who shares a life vision and is as invested in their spouse's career choices as they are in their own. That is exponentially beneficial to both.

Avivah Wittenberg-Cox is CEO of 20-first, one of the world's leading gender consulting firms, and author of *Seven Steps to Leading a Gender-Balanced Business*.

CHAPTER 16

Balance Parenting and Work Stress

by Daisy Wademan Dowling

"Ask for a flexible schedule—it's the only way to balance work and family."

"Think hard about part-time. You'll end up working on your days off anyway—for less money."

"Back in '86, when my first daughter was born, I learned to completely check out on evenings and weekends."

"Hire more help!"

"It only gets harder as they get older."

Most working parents look to their networks of mentors, coworkers, and professional contacts for advice on

---

Adapted from "Balancing Parenting and Work Stress: A Guide" on hbr.org, March 9, 2017 (product #H03IGQ).

balancing the competing demands of work and home. But the off-the-cuff guidance that most new working parents get, even if it's candid and well intentioned, isn't always helpful. Too often it's contradictory, vague, out of date, unactionable, even downright disheartening. With so many professional fathers and mothers depending on this common wisdom, it's no wonder workforce opt-out rates aren't budging and so many working parents report feeling exhausted and overwhelmed. Although it's a go-to resource, the working-parent grapevine doesn't always provide the most useful or can-do support.

Fortunately for professional parents, and for any leader looking to assist working-parent employees in a cost-effective way, there is advice that works: simple, universally applicable, no-fail recommendations that motivate and improve performance—fast.

Over the past decade of leading human capital, diversity, and retention efforts in several demanding US-based companies, I've spoken with hundreds of high-performing working parents and, in the hunt for real, feasible solutions, asked the same questions again and again: What advice has been the most valuable to you over the long term as a working parent? What specific action(s) can working fathers and mothers take to meet the demands of, and be comfortable in, their dual roles? What effective tricks and techniques do you wish you had known when you became a working parent?

What I've heard back is unexpected, empowering advice that addresses some of the greatest working-parent problems head-on and is universally relevant, too. It's as applicable for fathers as for mothers, whatever the family configuration, and regardless of roles or resources. These pieces of advice have helped "move the numbers" as part of broadscale corporate retention programs I've developed. They've worked for the individual professionals I've coached. They've been invaluable for me personally as a full-time working mother of two. And they will work for you, your people, and your organization.

Use Your Leading Professional Strengths

Whatever skills and traits have made you successful at work (organization? creativity? resilience? the ability to assemble a team?) will enable your success as a working parent. A strong organizer juggles the myriad demands and endless details of their dual role effectively with task lists on their phone; the creative thinker comes up with an unusual but happy childcare arrangement that accommodates their frequent last-minute business travel. Think about what you do best and most naturally on the job, take confidence in that strength, and then deploy it, hard, to meet your working-parent challenges.

Have a Vision of What You Want Working-Parent Life to Be—and Lead To

As in any business, having a defined mission and clear goals enable you to set priorities, align resources, measure success, and be confident you're on the right path. Every working parent is different. Your vision might be to "grow this business at double-digit rates while spending two hours a day with my kids" or "make partner while ensuring my children grow into healthy, self-sufficient adults" or "save enough to cover college while never missing a soccer game" or something else entirely. But whatever it consists of, having that view gives you the feeling of being in the driver's seat—and gives you confidence in your daily decisions.

Work Differently

Invest significant time in training and mentoring a junior colleague so they can run the budget meetings without you. Make friends in the business development team so that you know about the big local client projects coming up and can volunteer for them early (no business travel!). Be as physically visible in the office as possible—taking the long way to the coffee machine—so colleagues consider you to be around and available, even when you're at the pediatrician's office again. Without ever compromising the quality of your work, you can get it done in a way that better fits the needs of your life outside the office.

Manage the Village

If it takes a village to raise a child, your job is to build and manage that village the same way you would a project team at work. Get enough people on the team, and make sure their skills are complementary. Communicate clear priorities and ensure the team can act reliably in your absence. Give clear feedback—and demonstrate appreciation for a job well done. And put the village on speed dial: Make sure all your child's caregivers and support are immediately and easily reachable.

Don't Always Be a Doer

High-performing employees instinctively want to roll up their sleeves and do; they thrive on being heroes. But thriving as a working parent involves unlearning this trait—and delegating and finding shortcuts whenever possible. Look at your calendar for a few minutes each Friday, and find three meetings or tasks you could have avoided, condensed, or passed off. The new trainee could have done a first draft of the marketing summary; the groceries could have come from an Amazon standing order. Make "Friday review" a habit, and you'll be able to shave hours off your weekly work, gaining meaningful peace of mind.

Bring Workplace Efficiency Home

If you're using a big whiteboard in the kitchen to keep track of your family calendar or relying on email traffic to coordinate to-do lists, you will fail or simply become too exhausted to keep up. The same kind of technologies that enable you to compete at work—the calendars, the shared work tools—should be used at home. Downloading "life hack" apps onto your phone can help you move from "overwhelmed and exhausted" to "busy but managing."

Have a Plan B—and Don't Wait for a Crisis to Use It

Caregivers get sick; flights home are delayed; clients make demands for work to be completed by tomorrow. So have needed backups ready, and, more important, rehearse them. Put the number for your company's backup childcare center into your phone, and time how long it takes to drive there. Keep an overnight bag packed and waiting for when your kids suddenly need to spend the night at grandma's. Try out the local babysitting service on a weekend, when you're available to oversee the sitter. An effective contingency plan lets you consistently deliver at work and at home—and reduces your stress significantly.

Think Long-Term to Stay in the Game

As a longtime corporate HR professional, I've seen way too many parents decide to leave their jobs, or simply psychologically check out of them, during crises. The baby's got the flu, the employee hasn't slept in three days, and the annual department budget is due to the CFO's office. The situation feels insurmountable and endless, and so, desperate for relief, the employee decides to make a drastic change and quits. The decision is human and eminently understandable (what working parent hasn't faced the same type of situation?). But resilient working parents constantly remind themselves that getting through immediate rough patches will lead to long-term payoffs. The baby will only have the flu for a week, and you want to be in this career you love for decades. The grueling business trip ends Thursday, but your example of commitment and hard work will stick with your kids forever. You will have to be at the office late every night this week, but you are creating financial stability for your family. This "short-term/long-term" thinking allows you to weather the toughest spots on the working-parent journey, stay in the game, and maintain your motivation. Repeat to yourself: *This hard part will be over soon, and my long-term payoff is coming.*

To Get Flexibility, Don't Ask—Sell

Telling the boss that working from home on Wednesdays would save enough commute time that you could deliver the weekly sales reports early is more compelling than simply asking to work from home because "it's a lot easier for me with the twins." As any successful salesperson knows, the best pitches always lead with customer benefits. (See section 3 to learn more about flexible work arrangements.)

Use the 5% Solution

Don't take drastic measures to achieve balance though, such as changing jobs or going part-time, your first response. Instead, try getting the flexibility you need by leaving the office early once every other week, ducking out for the occasional soccer game, or going straight home from any flight that lands after 2 p.m. These measures sound small, and they are. They won't change your schedule more than 5%, they won't be enough to affect performance, and your boss may not even notice. But they will provide you enough feeling of flexibility and "give" to continue on your chosen path. Small-bite, self-directed, informal flexibility works just as well, and sometimes better, than a formal arrangement.

Working parenthood is a tough managerial, leadership, and personal challenge for anyone, regardless of how gifted or hard-working they are—and it lasts for a full 18 years, or more. Like most other big business problems, it has no silver bullet, no magically permanent fix. But whether you're a new working parent or a leader seeking to motivate and retain the working parents on your team, listening to others' specific solutions will help to create viable options of your own.

Daisy Wademan Dowling is the founder and CEO of Workparent, a consulting firm that provides practical, commercial advice, solutions, and training to working parents and to the organizations that employ them. She has led successful human-capital strategy, leadership development, and diversity efforts within several *Fortune* 500 companies—and now works as coach, consultant, and advisor to a broad range of organizations seeking to drive performance through their people. She can be reached through www.workparent.com.

CHAPTER 17

How Working Parents Can Manage the Demands of School-Age Kids

by Daisy Wademan Dowling

For working parents with school-age children, June is especially chaotic. The season brings end-of-the-school-year projects, state testing, report cards, parent-teacher conferences, the transition to 10 long weeks of child-care arrangements, the awkwardness of explaining to colleagues why you're out of the office *again*, the need

---

Adapted from content posted on hbr.org, June 13, 2018 (product #H04DW0).

to follow up with the pediatrician about health forms for September (they're overdue already), and the worry about whether your child will do better in math next year with a different teacher.

Your task list is endless, your stress level high. And a lot of the work and worry seems to be coming from one place: your child's school.

As a working parent, you've already got two jobs—and having two jobs isn't easy. But you're also going to spend a minimum of 13 years with a third critical role: stewarding your child's education. It's a position that comes with enormous hope and pressure. You want the absolute best for your children, and you're determined to oversee their school experience in a way that will set them up for success in college and life beyond. But it's a position that can create significant practical challenges for any family.

But here's the good news: There *are* effective ways to manage the overwhelming demands of drop-off, homework, and parent-teacher conferences while still delivering and succeeding at work.

Here, gleaned from teachers, school administrators, and experienced parents themselves, are a few of the simple, specific techniques that put any working parent of school-age kids on their front foot—and they'll work for your family, too.

Explain the *Why*, Not Just the When, of Time Away from Work

Instead of telling your boss and colleagues that you'll be "out of the office tomorrow afternoon," explain that "I'll be leaving the office tomorrow afternoon for two hours for a parent-teacher meeting at Brandon's school. We've been concerned about his math scores, and we're talking with the teacher about how to support him over the summer and into next year. I'll be back online by 6 p.m., and we can go over the budget draft at tomorrow's meeting." The second statement makes it vastly easier for colleagues to understand, sympathize, and ally themselves with you—and does a better job of telegraphing your commitment to the job as well. (See more on communicating about conflicts in chapter 18.)

Plan and Bundle Volunteer Commitments

Even with a very flexible job, it's unlikely that any working parent can make it to every bake sale, library fundraiser, and field trip. Here's what you do: In the first week of school, tell your child's teachers and/or the school's volunteer coordinators that you're eager to do your fair share—but that you will be doing it all in one go. You'll schedule a personal or vacation day well in advance and use it entirely for school volunteerism. Maybe you'll be the "reading helper" in your daughter's second-grade class in the morning, walk the school's neighborhood safety patrol in the afternoon, and take the minutes during the PTA fundraising committee meeting at 5 p.m. When the day is over, enjoy knowing that your yearly contribution has been made in full—and efficiently.

Invest Your Time Where It Matters Most

All working parents have packed schedules, yet "in our desire to fully engage with our children's education, many of us gravitate to time-intensive activities that may not actually have much impact on their success in school," says Ariela Rozman, a leading K–12 education expert and founding partner of EdNavigator, a not-for-profit that provides custom coaching and tools for parents seeking to keep their children on track in school. Rozman adds: "There may be great reasons for you to take part in school fundraising, attend school events, or help your child with their homework each evening. Maybe you want to support the school community or simply to spend time together with your kid. But think about putting some time toward the things that are proven to produce great results too." Rozman cites "The Broken Compass," a groundbreaking and comprehensive research study done by professors from the University of Texas and Duke University. They found that a handful of habits that make a real difference, such as reading aloud to young kids and talking to teenagers about college plans.

Make "Family Study Hall" a Habit

Beat the nightly homework drama (the nagging, the power struggles, the bargaining, the tears) by setting a hard-and-fast time each evening that the whole family has study hall: silent, dedicated work time around the dining table. The kids do their homework and you catch up on office emails or reading. When the kitchen timer rings, study hall is over, and the whole family gets to enjoy downtime or a relaxing activity like watching a favorite TV program together. This routine may not be easy for the first few nights you try it, but the kids will quickly adjust, and the benefits are many. They will learn how to focus better, to work more efficiently, and to use the "sprint and recover" approach when tackling a large workload—all skills that will make them more successful and happier in school and in their futures. You'll also have established a clear boundary between work and play—something that's vital and healthy for the entire family in our always-on world.

Treat Teachers and Administrators as You Would Valued Colleagues (Because That's What They Are)

For many parents, the parent-teacher relationship is fraught and unclear: Is the teacher an all-powerful evaluator, capable of changing your child's future with a few strokes of a red pen? Or a vendor who needs to be constantly nudged if you're going to get decent service? Will there be terrible consequences for your child if you dial into a parent-teacher meeting while on a business trip? The answer to all of those is no—but you do need to develop strong working relationships with the professionals teaching your child. To do so, think of a favorite coworker, one who you enjoy being staffed with on tough projects. The coworker is someone you constantly communicate with, sharing all critical information; someone you greet setbacks and roadblocks with by saying, "Let's figure out how to solve this together"; someone whose constructive comments you take graciously, offering your own in a spirit of respect, trust, and good humor. Take this exact same approach with educators: Tell Mrs. Wilson that you'll be away on business next week, in case your third-grader acts out; flag it when Susie is struggling with her Spanish homework—and ask what the best way is to support her; let the science teacher know your son loved the chemistry experiment. Teachers are professionals—and humans. They'll notice and appreciate your collaboration, and likely respond in kind.

Remember What You're Managing Toward

School, with all of its deadlines, complexity, evaluations, and social pressures, can be a daunting experience, for kids and for their parents. Amid all the noise and busyness, it can be helpful to re-center by remembering the two key outcomes you—and every parent—are really shooting for: independence and opportunity. You want your son or daughter to develop into a competent, responsible adult capable of managing in a complex world. And you want them to find the maximum possible number of open doors in terms of college and, later, in terms of career. But you don't need to ensure your child has a flawless, completely bump-and-bruise-free experience at school in order to get there. It's OK—desirable, even—for your child to struggle with long division or have an argument on the playground, or for you to miss a few soccer games. These things may be upsetting in the moment, particularly to you as a high-achieving professional, but they're the experiences your child needs to become resilient, independent, and ultimately successful in their own right.

Parenting school-age children while making it happen in a full-time career can feel like an uphill marathon of a task—long, constant, and steep. But remember: School won't be the only place your child gets their education. Like all parents, you will teach your child the greatest lessons: the importance of hard work, the value of commitments to family, and the satisfaction that comes from a tough job well done.

Daisy Wademan Dowling is the founder and CEO of Workparent, a consulting firm that provides practical, commercial advice, solutions and training to working parents and to the organizations that employ them. She has led successful human-capital strategy, leadership development, and diversity efforts within several *Fortune* 500 companies—and now works as coach, consultant and advisor to a broad range of organizations seeking to drive performance through their people. She can be reached through www.workparent.com.

CHAPTER 18

Keep Your Home Life Sane When Work Gets Crazy

by Stewart D. Friedman

When you're going through a phase that compels you to put more time, effort, brainpower, and heart into your job, how do you work it out with your family and others who matter in your life? And how do you make sure this spike in your focus on work doesn't become a "new normal" that extends indefinitely into the future? The short answer: Dialogue about what matters most—to you and to them.

First, forget *balance*, which is a misguided metaphor for what success looks like in the different parts of life.

Adapted from content posted on hbr.org, February 23, 2015 (product #H01W2T).

It's not possible to have perfect equilibrium among the four domains of life—work, home, community, and self—every day, every week, or even every year. Naturally, there are times when any one of these aspects of your life has to take center stage.

When a spike in work-related activities is having a deleterious effect on your family or on some other part of your life, then it's time for what I call "stakeholder dialogues"—conversations with the people who matter most about your mutual expectations and how best to meet them, now and in the long run.

Here are five steps to take in such conversations:

1. **Provide context** by letting people at home (or in your community) know why your work temporarily demands your attention to an extraordinary degree. As in "Let me give you a bit of background about what's happening . . ." Keep it short. This is not an excuse, just a brief explanation to set the stage for dialogue.

2. **Explain the purpose** of what you're doing at work and why you believe it's important, not solely for your own growth but for the positive impact you hope to have on others. As in, "By my devoting this effort now I'll be able to____, which is important to us because it'll help us to___."

3. **Ask about the consequences** they believe will result from this shift in your attention toward work. Learn more about what this adjustment means for them. As in, "Can you tell me how this

will make things harder for you?" and then follow up with "Can you give me an example?" Do not try to minimize the difficulties they report; instead, compassionately inquire.

4. **Express genuine remorse** for disappointments or hurt you might be causing, being specific about your understanding of how your actions are creating stresses and strains. As in "I'm sorry that my being unavailable is hurting you." Own it.

5. **Explore possible alternatives** for how you might minimize these negative effects. As in "I'm not sure what might help, but do you have ideas for what I can do to try to make this better for us, our family, our relationship?" And ask again, as in "What other thoughts do you have about what I can do, either now or sometime in the future?"

You're likely to discover possibilities for actions you can take that won't cost you much, but will help to minimize any damage caused by your work spike. You might even improve the quality of your relationships with your family, friends, and others in your life.

Assuming that if you're not home for dinner that your family is losing out, or that you're losing out, may not be an accurate read. Maybe driving your daughter to school is more important to her than your being home for dinner. Your spouse might be happy to meet you in town for dinner, even if you have to return to the office while he or she heads home afterward. Maybe they don't care so much if your travel increases or the length of your workday increases, as long as they have your *undivided* attention when you are at home. You won't know until you ask.

What I've found is that what others expect of you is usually a bit less than, and somewhat different from, what you think they expect of you. And unless you know what's essential and meaningful to them, now and in the future, you can't generate creative solutions that make sense for all of you.

Once you've navigated your way through an especially tumultuous episode at work and managed to keep your domestic ship of state on course, it's useful to again be deliberate in choosing a path forward that suits all parties. You might want to mark the end of that period as a special occasion with a celebratory dinner, as a way of closing the book on it.

Then, keep your stakeholder dialogues going as you return to a normal workload. Take a bit of time to review which of the strategies you employed worked well and which did not. The key is remaining open to discovering new ways of adjusting—either at work or at home—that let you pursue what you care about most, no matter what the world throws at you.

Stewart D. Friedman is the Professor of Management Practice Emeritus at the Wharton School. The former head of Ford Motor's Leadership Development Center, he is the author of *Leading the Life You Want: Skills for*

Integrating Work and Life, *Baby Bust: New Choices for Men and Women in Work and Family*, and *Total Leadership: Be a Better Leader, Have a Richer Life*. For more, visit www.totalleadership.org, or find him on Twitter @StewFriedman or on LinkedIn.

SECTION FIVE

Take Care of Yourself

CHAPTER 19

Six Ways to Weave Self-Care into Your Workday

by Amy Jen Su

I've spent the past few years working closely with leaders on incorporating self-care into their work lives—as a key component of their overall performance—so that an expansion in their role or responsibilities doesn't come at the expense of their health and well-being. One CEO I worked with summed it up best when he said: "Self-care is no longer a luxury; it's part of the job."

So, what exactly *is* self-care, and how do we do it?

Adapted from content posted on hbr.org, June 19, 2017 (product #H03QHM).

Define Self-Care More Broadly

At the heart of self-care is your relationship and connection to self. As part of your job, it means that you're attuned to and understand what you need to be your most constructive, effective, and authentic self. Therefore, rather than narrowly defining self-care as just physical health (which is an important piece of the equation), we need to pay attention to a wider set of criteria, including care of the mind, emotions, relationships, environment, time, and resources.

Take Out the Word "Should"

Self-care can feel daunting or unattainable. But the intention is not to add more to your already full plate, or create a reason to beat yourself up. For example, you might find yourself annoyed when someone suggests that you need to take better care of yourself, especially when it seems they don't understand how much you've already got on your plate. Self-care doesn't originate from judgment and isn't reactive to judgment (both are forms of self-sabotage, as I describe later). Instead, self-care flows from an intention to stay connected to oneself and one's overall mission: *Who and what can support and be in service of the positive contribution I hope to make?*

Work Self-Care into Your Day-to-Day Work

Rather than having self-care be something "outside" of work, it's important to weave it naturally into the course of your workday. Below are six ways I've seen clients take purposeful action. Self-care is highly personal, though, so rather than being an exhaustive list, these ideas are meant to get your gears turning.

Cut yourself a break

We can often be our own harshest critic. When the weight of accountability or perfectionism kicks in, ask yourself: "What would I say to a colleague or friend in the same situation?" Research from HBS professor Amy Edmondson has shown that we optimize performance and learning in groups when both accountability and psychological safety are present. These principles can also help you as an individual. By keeping your internal critic at bay, you can create the right psychological conditions to accelerate through periods of rumination or self-doubt more quickly.

Value time, money, and resources

Throughout a given workday, others frequently ask for our time or resources, distracting us from more important priorities. That's why it's important to set aside 15 minutes first thing each morning to jot down the three things you hope to accomplish that day. Then, as requests come in, consider the impact on your priorities before offering a knee-jerk automatic yes. For those who are self-employed, the same goes when you are asked about your fees and services. Self-care means honoring the value, impact, and contribution you bring.

Take a victory lap

What did you do last week? Most of us can't remember because once we've completed a deliverable or gotten through a tough crunch, we've already moved on to the next thing. Instead, hit the pause button with yourself and your team to take a look back at the previous month or quarter, and name or write down what went well or what felt particularly satisfying. This kind of debrief can help you and your team stay connected to passions, highest contributions, and actions that actually add value.

Surround yourself with good people

Healthy and supportive relationships are a critical part of self-care. Consider whether your team is providing ample leverage and support to meet priorities. Take notice of who feeds your energy and who drains it. Set more boundaries with the drainers. Invest in those who inspire and support you and who understand what it means to have a healthy give and take. The same goes for your relationships outside of work. Don't let work cause you to neglect the most important people in your life. Use breaks during the day, or perhaps your commute time, to call friends and loved ones and carve out plenty of time outside of work to nurture relationships.

Update your workspace

Our environment and workspace can have a significant impact on productivity. Gain more mental clarity by cleaning up your desk. Put up pictures, artwork, or images that inspire you or remind you of the people and things that matter. Your workspace should feel like a reflection of your best self.

Recharge and reboot

Stay attuned to your energy levels. For most busy professionals, getting eight hours of sleep every night is (sadly) not realistic. But it's important to at least try to refill your gas tank during the week, so designate a Wednesday or Thursday night to get in some extra sleep. And it's equally important to build restoration breaks into your workday. For example, try scheduling more walking meetings, or make a point of having lunch away from your desk with a colleague or friend. If you're traveling for work and find yourself with an extra 30 minutes before boarding a flight, stop by one of the airport massage stands to relax and recharge before your trip.

Notice When You've Slipped Out of Self-Care Mode

In times of stress, self-care can get especially off-balance. Be aware, with self-compassion, of when you've lost touch with your authentic self in one of the following ways.

Self-neglect

With demanding workloads and overly full plates, self-neglect can become a familiar pattern for many of us. It feels like we're always running on a hamster wheel. As feelings of anxiety and being overwhelmed increase, it becomes harder to maintain composure and say no to the daily fire drills, interruptions, and demands of others. We end our workdays feeling completely burned out.

Self-management

Maintaining a professional and competent persona is an important leadership skill, but in some cases, we can take it too far. When you overly manage yourself, you suppress or deny emotion, working hard to uphold a professional game face. You end up feeling exhausted from keeping up the act and risk being perceived as inauthentic.

Self-sabotage

Sometimes, we don't achieve our mission or highest priorities because we have gotten in our own way. Notice when you have slipped into unproductive habits of procrastination, rumination, or distraction to avoid the anxiety or fear of completing your most important tasks.

Self-preservation

In a competitive world, it's easy to succumb to a scarcity mindset. When we're focused on a lack of resources, we can lose touch with what's best for the business. Being competitive can cause others to perceive you as overly protective of your own turf and being in it for yourself.

In each of these cases, we are no longer in the driver's seat. Instead, anxiety, control, disdain of vulnerability, or fear is running the show. Notice, without judgment, when you've slipped into one of these places, and then gently reach for a self-care action to come back to yourself more fully.

As our work lives only get busier, self-care will become an ever more important part of being authentic and having a positive impact without sacrificing our health or relationships. By incorporating self-care in our day-to-day work lives—and coming back to it in times of stress—we can all become our most constructive, effective, and authentic selves.

Amy Jen Su is a cofounder and managing partner of Paravis Partners, a boutique executive coaching and leadership development firm. She is coauthor, with Muriel Maignan Wilkins, of *Own the Room: Discover Your Signature Voice to Master Your Leadership Presence.* Follow Amy on twitter @amyjensu.

CHAPTER 20

The Difference Between Workaholics and Working Long Hours

by Lieke ten Brummelhuis and Nancy P. Rothbard

Hanna, a finance director at an international home care retailer, works long hours. She's usually in the office from 9 a.m. to 5 p.m., but at home, when her three children

---

Adapted from "How Being a Workaholic Differs from Working Long Hours—and Why That Matters for Your Health" on hbr.org, March 22, 2018 (product #H048GE).

go to sleep, she'll work another four hours, not closing her laptop until midnight. She sometimes also works on weekends. But even though she works 60 to 65 hours per week, she told us that she can "switch off" when she needs to, and that she still feels energetic every day. She hasn't had to worry about her health.

Michael, the director of strategy for an American insurance company, does not work as much as Hanna. His workdays usually start at 8 a.m. and finish no later than 6 p.m., and he often leaves work at 3 p.m. on Fridays. But even though he works an average of 45 hours a week and is single with no kids, he has a hard time "switching off" and unwinding from his job—he is constantly checking his email and worrying about work. A few months ago, at a routine health check, his doctor noted he had high LDL cholesterol, which raises his risk for cardiovascular disease and diabetes. He was prescribed medication to lower it.

We generally assume that working too much is bad for our health. But what exactly is unhealthy about overwork is unclear. Is it working long hours that increases our risk of developing health issues? Or is it something else, like Michael's compulsive work mentality, that is harmful to our health?

What Our Research Shows

We sought to unravel the difference between behavior (working long hours) and mentality (a compulsion to work, or what we call workaholism). We conducted a study in 2010 at the Dutch subsidiary of an international financial consulting firm with over 3,500 employees.

WHAT IS WORKAHOLISM?

The term "workaholic" was coined in 1971 by the psychologist Wayne E. Oates, who referred to "an uncontrollable need to work incessantly" as an addiction. Workaholics are characterized by having an inner compulsive drive to work hard, thinking about work constantly, and feeling guilty and restless when they are not working. Workaholism often goes hand in hand with working long hours, but the two are distinct: It's possible to work long hours without being obsessed with work, and it is possible to be obsessed with work but only work 35 hours a week or less.

We asked employees to complete a survey and then sign up for a health screening conducted by medical staff; 763 employees completed both.

The survey asked about participants' workaholic tendencies (for example, "I feel guilty when I am not working on something" or "I put myself under pressure with self-imposed deadlines when I work"), their work skills, work motivation, and their work hours in an average week. It also asked if they experienced various psychosomatic health issues, such as headaches and stomach problems. The health screenings gave us information about their various biomarkers (such as waist measurement, triglycerides, blood pressure, and cholesterol), which, when aggregated, are a reliable gauge for an employee's risk of developing cardiovascular diseases and diabetes—what is referred to as Risk for Metabolic Syndrome (RMS). We also controlled for a host of factors such as gender, age, education, and family history of cardiovascular disease.

We found that work hours were not related to any health issues, while workaholism was. Specifically, employees who worked long hours (typically more than 40 hours a week) but who did not obsess about work did not have increased levels of RMS and reported fewer health complaints than employees who demonstrated workaholism. We found that workaholics, whether or not they worked long hours, reported more health complaints and had increased risk for metabolic syndrome; they also reported a higher need for recovery, more sleep problems, more cynicism, more emotional exhaustion, and more depressive feelings than employees who merely worked long hours but did not have workaholic tendencies.

The experiences of Hanna and Michael, individuals whom we interviewed separately, outside of this study, align with these results. Hanna works long hours, but she is not mentally preoccupied with work. When she finishes work for the night, she feels fulfilled and falls asleep easily. In the morning, she feels refreshed for a new workday. She told us, "I take my work very seriously while I'm working, but I forget about work the minute I decide I've done enough for the day." Michael, on the other hand, has a compulsion to work hard and feels restless when he is not working. He continues to ruminate about his job and often finds it difficult to fall asleep and recharge before the next morning. When asked about his general stress levels, he mentioned that he "cannot remember the last time not feeling stressed or anxious about work."

Unlike people who merely work long hours, workaholics struggle to psychologically detach from work. And we know that ongoing rumination often goes together with stress, anxiety, depression, and sleep problems, and it impedes recovery from work. Stress levels in workaholics are therefore often chronic, which leads to ongoing wear and tear on the body.

Here's a quick explanation of why: To cope with stress, the body activates several systems (for example, cardiovascular, neuroendocrine). So say you're facing an important deadline. As you approach it, your stress hormones (such as cortisol), pro- and anti-inflammatory cytokines (for example, interleukin-6), and blood pressure would likely go up. But after the deadline, these would return to their original levels, known as the "set points." When you're working an excessive workload and continually pushing your system beyond its range, you may reset your set points. Elevated blood pressure may become chronic, and cortisol levels stay elevated. When your biological systems keep working around elevated set points, you have a greater risk of cardiovascular disease (CVD), diabetes, and even death.

Does It Matter If You Love the Work?

Most workaholics are aware of their obsessive work habits, and friends and family will often warn them about the possible health risks. But a common defense is that they love their jobs. Linda, a personal injury lawyer whom we also interviewed separately from our study, readily admits to her work addiction but says she simply enjoys her work too much to change. Linda works for a medium-sized law firm in Canada. Although her hours are exceptionally low for a lawyer (40 hours per week), she feels guilty when she is not working and often tries to come up with solutions for her clients off the job. As a result, she finds it difficult to fully engage in play with her five-year-old after work. She often experiences headaches and difficulty sleeping, as she ruminates about work and thinks up new ways of tackling work challenges. When talking to her husband and a trusted colleague about the ongoing headaches and sleep problems, they both urged her to visit the doctor but she initially resisted. She told us, "There is really not much wrong with me, at least not physically. I just need more hours in the day."

We wanted to see if enjoying the work mitigates the negative health effects of workaholism. Looking at the data from our study, we differentiated between workaholics who reported being highly engaged with their work—meaning they enjoyed their work, felt vigorous at work, and got easily absorbed in their work—and workaholics who reported low work engagement. We found that both types of workaholics reported more psychosomatic health complaints (for example, headache, stomach problems) and mental health complaints (sleep problems, depressive feelings) than non-workaholics. However, non-engaged workaholics had higher RMS—a 4.2% higher risk—than engaged workaholics. (This number might seem small, but even a small increase can pose a serious health risk.)

This suggests that loving your work can mitigate some of the risk associated with obsessing over it. We also found that engaged workaholics reported having more resources at home and at work compared to nonengaged workaholics. Engaged workaholics reported receiving more social support (for example, advice, information, appreciation), from their supervisor, coworkers, and their spouse, than their nonengaged counterparts. They also scored higher on communication skills, time management skills, and general work skills, and they reported much higher intrinsic motivation for work than nonengaged workaholics.

We think that this arsenal of resources may help engaged workaholics prevent initial health complaints from developing into more severe health risks. In Linda's case, after listening to her husband's concerns, she eventually consulted her doctor. The doctor did a general health check, and as Linda suspected, the results did not reveal any concerns in terms of physiological health. But her doctor referred her to a counselor to work on the sleep problems Linda mentioned during the checkup.

If we look at all of our examples, it's clear that while Hanna, Michael, and Linda all work hard, the way they engage with work differs substantially, and hence, their health risk differs as well. Due to Hanna's long work hours, her stress levels are high at times, but because they return to baseline levels, her stress is not chronic and she does not have the related mental or physical health risks. Michael has an obsessive work mentality, and he does not enjoy his work, which causes ongoing stress and frustration, frequent anxiety attacks and feelings of depression, and also elevated risk for cardiovascular disease. Linda has a similar compulsive work mentality, but she loves her job and reports having a supportive family. While she experiences some sleep issues and headaches, she does not have an elevated risk for cardiovascular diseases.

Two Key Messages—and Their Caveats

These stories and our research findings reveal two key messages: First, when it comes to effects on health, working long hours is not as bad as obsessing over work. But this warrants an important disclaimer: The employees in our sample worked a maximum of 65 hours per week, and therefore we do not know the health outcomes of working longer hours. It may be quite difficult to detach from work, engage in recovery activities, or get enough sleep if one works 70 hours per week or more. Still, it seems that more than hours, our thoughts and feelings about work impact our subjective well-being and health risks.

The second key message from our study is that workaholics who love their jobs are somewhat protected from the most severe health risks, and this may be because they feel that their work is worth all the hard work they put in. But this brings up another caveat: Although we found that engaged workaholics had lower physiological health risks (lower RMS) than nonengaged workaholics, they still reported more depressive feelings, sleep problems, various psychosomatic health complaints, and a higher need for recovery than nonworkaholics. These are all signs that well-being among workaholics, regardless of how much they love their job, can be impaired.

Avoiding the Negative Effects of Workaholism

Our research suggests some potential solutions to help keep stress levels manageable and prevent health risks. The first step is to acknowledge when a relationship to work is unhealthy—when it feels out of control and is undermining outside relationships. The next step is to regain control over your work behavior. One way to do this is by setting clear rules for how many hours you will work each day. This can help you accept that there is a point at which you've done enough work for the day. If you have trouble "switching off," you might want to stop working two or three hours before bed. Taking up enjoyable nonwork activities, such as seeing friends, watching a movie, reading a book, or learning a new skill, can also help you psychologically detach from work.

It can also be useful to reflect on the reasons why you work excessively and compulsively. We found a striking difference in work motivation between engaged and nonengaged workaholics. Whereas engaged workaholics worked because they enjoyed their work or found their work meaningful (these are intrinsic motivators), nonengaged workaholics were more likely to work for extrinsic motivators such as money and status. Intrinsic motivation is associated with more optimism, effort, and persistence, whereas extrinsic motivation often instigates anxiety and undermines persistence, making failure more likely.

ARE YOU OBSESSIVELY PASSIONATE ABOUT YOUR WORK?

by Scott Barry Kaufman

Work brings some people intrinsic joy. These people feel in control of their work, feel good about themselves while working, find their work to be in harmony with their other activities. Psychologists describe these folks as having *harmonious passion*. But there's another kind of passion: *obsessive passion*. Those who are obsessively passionate feel an uncontrollable urge to engage in their work, feel more conflict between their passion and other areas in their life, and their work forms a large part of their often unstable and negative self-concept.

How can you tell if your passion for work is obsessive? There are clear warning signs; here are some questions to ask yourself.

- ***Do you have enough energy?*** Do you engage in your work with positive enthusiasm? Do you feel enjoyment doing what you do?
- ***Do you define yourself by criteria other than work?*** If your self is a pie, how big of a bite does your work take out of it?
- ***Do you have a positive self-image?*** Obsessive passion is correlated with a negative image of the self, including automatic subconscious

associations between the self and the concept "unpleasant."

- ***When you work, is your interior monologue positive?*** Is it filled with words like "want to," "get to," and "can't wait to"? Or are words like "must," "need," and "have to" rattling around?
- ***Are you able to stop working when you want to?*** Recent research found that online gamers who were very harmoniously passionate about gaming felt positive emotions while playing, while gamers with obsessive passion felt more negative emotions both when playing *and when prevented from playing*. Do you feel a compulsion to work all the time, even when you really don't want to?
- ***Do you get into a state of flow?*** Do you feel as though time has receded into the background, or do you feel the weight of pressure on your back? Flow is an enjoyable experience, whereas obsessive engagement feels more urgent.

If you're reading down that list and thinking, "no, no, no," these are signs that you may have obsessive, not harmonious, passion. If you do think your level of obsessive passion might be too high, there are some things you can do about it.

(*continued*)

ARE YOU OBSESSIVELY PASSIONATE ABOUT YOUR WORK?

- ***Schedule real breaks.*** If you recognize you're obsessively passionate about your work, force yourself to get out of that headspace by scheduling other activities during the course of the day (like lunch with a friend or a break to hit the gym). Block out time after work or on weekends for family, friends, and activities you enjoy. Having a schedule will keep you honest.
- ***Don't bring work home.*** If you can afford to, make it completely impossible to access your work once you leave work. Don't bring home your laptop. Leave those files on your desk. Keep separate email accounts for home and work, and don't check work email when you're at home (put up an out-of-office message if you have to). Obsessive passion is really just a bad habit, and habits can be broken gently.
- ***Change your thought patterns when you work.*** Fake the mindset of the harmoniously passionate person until you make it. For instance, convert thoughts of "must" and "need" to "want" and "desire." At first, this may feel awkward, but eventually the obsessively pas-

sionate mindset will dissipate, and so will the behaviors associated with it. A recent study suggests that changing your explicit thought patterns may increase self-esteem and harmonious passion.

- ***Commit to a new hobby.*** Often, investing too much self in one project is an indication of a negative core self. The more additional things outside of work contribute to a positive sense of self, the less space your work performance will take up in your ego, and the smaller your chances of burnout.

Scott Barry Kaufman is a psychologist at Barnard College, Columbia University. He is the author of *Ungifted: Intelligence Redefined* and coauthor of *Wired to Create: Unraveling the Mysteries of the Creative Mind* (with Carolyn Gregoire). Kaufman also writes a column for *Scientific American* and hosts *The Psychology Podcast*.

Adapted from "Increase Your Passion for Work Without Becoming Obsessed" on hbr.org, September 21, 2011.

The proactive mentality that is characteristic of employees with intrinsic motivation may help them take action when they experience initial health complaints, whereas the anxiety and frustration that can accompany extrinsic motivation may make nonengaged workaholics more passive, such that they continue unhealthy work habits and eventually face substantial health risks. Thus, finding ways to promote intrinsic motivation in one's work, whether through new projects or even a new job, may not only make you happier but also healthier.

Managers too can intervene by helping employees find intrinsic motivation; they can promote their re-engagement in their work and provide more support. This can mean assigning employees challenging but feasible tasks, reducing red tape and other barriers, discussing their personal and professional growth, and providing them with ample resources to do their work, such as autonomy, feedback, and support. Managers can help hard workers develop stronger communication and time management skills, with tactics such as making a to-do list each week, compiling a long-term goal list, differentiating between urgent and nonurgent tasks, and scheduling uninterrupted time for important tasks. Friends and family can also play a role by making sure that employees have emotional and tangible support at home.

Ultimately, the challenge is to identify one's own compulsive work mentality and prevent its consequences. Focusing on one's engagement and ability to "switch off" will go a long way in helping employees feel happy at work and outside of it.

Lieke ten Brummelhuis is an assistant professor of management at the Beedie School of Business, Simon Fraser University. She received her PhD in organizational sociology from Utrecht University in the Netherlands. Lieke is interested in research topics related to employee well-being including work-life balance, stress, workaholism, recovery, and health. **Nancy P. Rothbard** is the David Pottruck Professor of Management at the Wharton School, University of Pennsylvania. She received hcr AB from Brown University and her PhD from the University of Michigan. Her research focuses on the interplay between emotions and engagement in multiple life roles and how people navigate the boundaries between them.

CHAPTER 21

How to Forget About Work When You're Not Working

by Art Markman

When was the last time you got away from work?

I mean truly got *away* from it: didn't think about it, didn't worry about it, didn't have a to-do list rattling around in your brain.

Most of us know there are benefits to getting away from work. We know we need time to recharge each day in order to be able to sustain our attention in the office.

Adapted from content posted on hbr.org, August 25, 2017 (product #H03V9X).

We know time away from complex problems allows us to find a fresh perspective. We know if we work too many long days in a row we'll find ourselves doing what I affectionately call "fake work"—sitting at our desks without actually accomplishing anything.

The hard part is that while you may agree with all of these benefits of getting away from your work, you may still have trouble doing it. Even if you do go home at a decent hour in the evening, you may find yourself reading one last report. When you travel for a few days, you may still be attached to your email. When you wake up early in the morning, or lie awake at night, you might find your brain sorting through a long list of work tasks. I have even known people who have had dreams about problems they are facing at work.

When we can't let go of work while we're out of the office, we don't get to enjoy the benefits of time away. To wean yourself off work—and unwanted thoughts of work—you can use a combination of new habits and lessons from cognitive behavioral therapy. Here's how.

Focus on What You'll Do Instead

Many people fail to change their behavior because they focus on what they are *not* going to do rather than on actions they will take instead. Setting the goal *not* to work (or think about work) when you are away from the office starts with the presumption that you will stop yourself every time you are tempted to do something work-related.

Negative goals like this—where you focus on actions you will no longer take—tend to fail for two reasons.

First, your habit system only learns a new habit when you perform an action, not when you don't. So you cannot create a habit to avoid an action. Second, when you set negative goals, you have to constantly be vigilant about your behavior. Otherwise, you will end up doing the thing you are trying to avoid.

Instead, you need to focus on what you are going to do *instead of working*. Create a plan for your time away from work—whether it is an evening out of the office or time on vacation. You need a specific plan, or you will return to your habits and re-engage with work when you should be away from it. The plan should focus on the activities you are going to perform instead of working.

For example, you might set up a personal training session for 5:30 p.m. at a gym near your office a couple of nights a week. Or you might tell your spouse that you'll pick up the kids at daycare. Or start volunteering at a local charity on the weekends. You can even do some personal development. Sign up for a class to learn a new language. Take up a musical instrument. Start painting. All of these activities will limit the time you have for work, and replace work with other pursuits.

Sometimes, though, your downtime may still be interrupted by intrusive thoughts about work. In this case, you want to be prepared so that you don't keep ruminating about upcoming work. (Ruminating is a great word, by the way; it comes from the word for cows chewing their cud.)

There are two ways to deal with intrusive thoughts. One is to have a plan to occupy your mind at the ready: Read a novel, do a crossword puzzle, or phone a friend.

However, there are times when there is something about work that really is bugging you. In that case, keep a notebook handy. Set a timer for 10 minutes and write down whatever is bothering you; this can help clear your mind. This is particularly true when the thoughts you are having about work reflect anxieties rather than simply the tasks you have to perform when you get back.

Change Your Environment

A smoker doesn't leave a large carton of cigarettes in their pantry while trying to quit smoking. Similarly, someone trying to set healthier work-life boundaries doesn't leave their phone and computer on all the time. Change your environment to support your new behavior and discourage the old one.

Yes, I am suggesting you turn your devices off. All the way off! A great way to manage the temptation to work when you are away from the office is to make it hard to do that work. If you have to switch your phone back on to check it, you might think twice before doing it.

You can also use the environment to help you if you often ruminate about work. Set up a space at home that you will never use to work. It could be a room, but it might also be a corner somewhere. Put a chair there (or a mat or a pillow). Use it as a place where you will engage in nonwork activities, like reading or yoga. The more that you associate this spot with things that do not involve work, the easier it will be to use this area to get away from work thoughts.

As part of creating this new, healthier environment, engage other people to help you. Ask your friends and family members to help you stay away from work. Give them permission to remind you to put your phone away (and don't get annoyed with them when they do). Find activities you can do with them that prevent you from working and that distract you from work-related thoughts.

Step Away from Work—and Watch Disaster *Not* Strike

Even if you do create these plans and an environment conducive to seeing them through, you still need to be *willing* to disconnect from work for a period of time. That can be anxiety-provoking. After all, you might miss an important email; something could go wrong; important work might be done badly or not done at all.

This is where a lesson from cognitive behavioral therapies may help. Studies suggest that a great way to reduce anxiety is to expose yourself to the scary situation and gradually learn that the situation is not actually threatening.

If your problem is that you're constantly worried about missing an important email, go a night without checking your email—and discover that all of the work you need to do is still there in the morning. Then expand the amount of time you leave your email unchecked. Try to get through an entire day of the weekend without checking. Then—gasp!—an entire weekend. You may find that many people manage to answer their own questions if you don't get back to them right away. On top of that, you will return to work with more energy and better ideas because you took some time off.

Art Markman, PhD, is the Annabel Irion Worsham Centennial Professor of Psychology and Marketing at the University of Texas at Austin and director of the IC2 Institute. He has written more than 150 scholarly papers on topics including reasoning, decision-making, and motivation. He is a cohost of the radio show and podcast *Two Guys on Your Head* and the author of several books including *Smart Thinking, Smart Change,* and B*rain Briefs*. His latest book is *Bring Your Brain to Work.*

CHAPTER 22

Regular Exercise Is Part of Your Job

by Ron Friedman

When we think about the value of exercise, we tend to focus on the physical benefits: lower blood pressure, a healthier heart, a more attractive physique. But over the past decade, social scientists have quietly amassed compelling evidence suggesting that there is another, more immediate benefit of regular exercise: its impact on the way we think.

Studies indicate that our mental firepower is directly linked to our physical regimen. And nowhere are the implications more relevant than to our performance at work. Consider the following cognitive benefits, all of

---

Adapted from content posted on hbr.org, October 3, 2014 (product #H01134).

which you can expect as a result of incorporating regular exercise into your routine:

- Improved concentration
- Sharper memory
- Faster learning
- Prolonged mental stamina
- Enhanced creativity
- Lower stress

Exercise has also been shown to elevate mood, which has serious implications for workplace performance. I'm willing to bet that your job requires you to make interpersonal connections and foster collaborations. Within this context, feeling irritable is no longer simply an inconvenience. It can directly influence the degree to which you are successful.

There is also evidence suggesting that exercise during *regular work hours* may boost performance. Take, for example, the results of a Leeds Metropolitan University study, which examined the influence of daytime exercise among office workers with access to a company gym. Many of us would love the convenience of free weights or a yoga studio at the office. But does using these amenities actually make a difference?

Within the study, researchers had over 200 employees at a variety of companies self-report their performance on a daily basis. They then examined fluctuations *within* individual employees, comparing their output on days when they exercised to days when they didn't.

Here's what they found: On days when employees visited the gym, their experience at work changed. They reported managing their time more effectively, being more productive, and having smoother interactions with their colleagues. Just as important: They went home feeling more satisfied at the end of the day.

What prevents us from exercising more often? For many of us, the answer is simple: We don't have the time. In fairness, this is a legitimate explanation. There are weeks when work is overwhelming and deadlines outside our control need to be met.

But let's be clear: What we really mean when we say we don't have time for an activity is that we don't consider it a priority given the time we have available.

This is why the research illuminating the cognitive benefits of exercise is so compelling. Exercise enables us to soak in more information, work more efficiently, and be more productive.

And yet many of us continue to perceive it as a luxury; an activity we'd *like* to do if only we had more time.

Instead of viewing exercise as something we do for ourselves—a personal indulgence that takes us away from our work—it's time we started considering physical activity as part of the work itself. The alternative, which involves processing information more slowly, forgetting more often, and getting easily frustrated, makes us less effective at our jobs and more difficult for our colleagues to get along with.

How do you successfully incorporate exercise into your routine? Here are a few research-based suggestions.

Identify a Physical Activity You Actually Like

There are many ways to work out other than boring yourself senseless on a treadmill. Find a physical activity you can look forward to doing, like tennis, swimming, dancing, softball, or even vigorously playing the drums. You are far more likely to stick with an activity if you genuinely enjoy doing it.

A series of recent studies also suggest that how we *feel* while exercising can influence the degree to which it ultimately benefits our health. When we view exercise as something we do for fun, we're better at resisting unhealthy foods afterwards. But when the same physical activity is perceived as a chore, we have a much harder time saying no to fattening foods, presumably because we've used up all of our willpower exercising.

Invest in Improving Your Performance

Instead of settling for "getting some exercise," focus on *mastering* an activity instead. Mastery goals, which psychologists define as goals that center on achieving new levels of competence, have consistently been shown to predict persistence across a wide range of domains. So hire a coach, enroll in a class, and buy yourself the right clothing and equipment. The additional financial investment will increase your level of commitment, while the steady gains in performance will help sustain your interest over the long haul.

Become Part of a *Group*, Not a *Collective*

One recommendation aspiring gym-goers often receive is to find an exercise regimen that involves other people. It's good advice. Socializing makes exercise more fun, which improves the chances that you'll keep doing it. It's also a lot harder to back out on a friend or a trainer than to persuade yourself that just one night off couldn't hurt.

But there's another layer to this research—one that is well worth considering before signing up for an exercise class.

Studies indicate that not all "group" activities are equally effective at sustaining our interest.

We are far more likely to stick with an exercise regimen when others are dependent on our participation.

As an illustration, consider the standard yoga or Pilates class. Each involves *individual-based tasks* that require you to work alone, albeit in the presence of others. Both activities technically take place within the context of a *group*. However, in these cases the "group" is more accurately described as a *collective*.

Research suggests that if you're looking to establish a routine that sticks, exercising as part of a collective is preferable to working out alone, but it's not nearly as effective as exercising as part of a team. So consider volleyball, soccer, doubles tennis—any enjoyable, competence-enhancing activity in which your efforts contribute directly to a team's success, and where if you don't show up, others will suffer.

Regardless of how you go about incorporating exercise into your routine, reframing it as part of your job makes it a lot easier to make time for it. Remember, you're not abandoning work. On the contrary: You're ensuring that the hours you put in have value.

Ron Friedman, PhD, is an award-winning psychologist and the founder of ignite80, a company that teaches leaders practical, evidence-based strategies for working smarter and creating thriving organizations. He is the author of *The Best Place to Work: The Art and Science of Creating an Extraordinary Workplace* and frequently delivers keynotes and workshops on the science of workplace excellence.

CHAPTER 23

Reclaim Your Commute

by Francesca Gino, Bradley Staats, Jon Jachimowicz, Julia Lee, and Jochen Menges

Every day, millions of people around the world face long commutes to work. In the United States alone, approximately 25 million workers spend more than 90 minutes each day getting to and from their jobs, and about 600,000 "mega-commuters" travel at least 90 minutes each way, according to the US Census Bureau. In the United Kingdom, the average round-trip commute takes 54 minutes (up from 45 minutes in 2003), and in most of the world's major cities, from Milan to Manila, it's over an hour.

Reprinted from *Harvard Business Review*, May–June 2017 (product #R1703M).

And yet few people enjoy their commutes. When Ford Motor Company surveyed 5,500 people in six European cities, many ranked commuting as more stressful than their jobs, moving into a new house, or going to the dentist. In a 2006 survey of 909 working women in Texas, conducted by Nobel laureate Daniel Kahneman and his colleagues, respondents said the morning journey between home and the office was, on average, the least enjoyable activity of their day; the evening trip home was the third worst. (Working itself took second place.)

This distaste for commuting has serious implications for well-being. A 2014 British government survey found that workers with lengthy commutes felt more anxious and less satisfied with life than people with shorter ones. They were also less likely to find their daily activities worthwhile. Other studies have found that people with long commutes are more exhausted and less productive at work, and have lower job satisfaction. And a study conducted in Sweden in 2011 found that couples have a 40% higher chance of getting divorced when one partner commutes at least 45 minutes to work each day.

But it doesn't have to be this way. Research, including our own studies, suggests that small tweaks can improve your commuting experience, leaving you happier and more productive. Here are five strategies to try.

Use the Time to Shift Your Mindset

Your commute is an opportunity to transition from the personal to the professional. At home in the morning, you might play the role of parent, partner, or caregiver. When you arrive at the office, you don your professional hat. In the evening, you might revert to the personal even if you eventually switch to finish up work before bed. Each of these transitions requires a shift in mindset. If we don't take the time to make one, the thoughts and concerns that stem from one role are likely to carry over into the next and weigh us down.

One way to smooth this mental transition is to engage in simple rituals. In an as-yet-unpublished study of regular commuters, one of us (Francesca) and Hal Hershfield of UCLA found that those who maintained small routines on the way to work—such as checking the news on the train or having a look at the calendar for the day—felt more excited about the day ahead, more satisfied with their jobs, and less stressed-out than those who had no set routine. This is not surprising, given that rituals have been shown to produce all sorts of benefits—even for people who don't believe in their value or effects: They lower our anxiety before we engage in high-stakes performance tasks, increase our enjoyment of the activity at hand, and even help us recover faster when we experience failure or loss. So consider establishing your own commuting routines. You might buy a decaf latte from the same coffee shop every day on your way to work, for example. For an even more powerful effect, try making a ritual out of one or more of the other commute-enhancing tactics we recommend below.

Prepare to Be Productive

When you spend at least some of your commute planning for the day or the week ahead, you'll arrive at work better prepared and therefore happier and more energetic and productive. That's what we concluded from a series of studies we did with British and American workers. The first was a field study of 225 employees at the UK offices of DigitasLBi, a global marketing and technology agency. As we expected, our study showed that, on average, the longer people commuted each day, the less content and more likely to quit they were. But there were exceptions to the rule, which left us wondering whether those individuals possessed certain psychological traits that helped them avoid the negative outcomes experienced by their peers. We found one: self-control, or the ability to resist temptations that can undermine efforts to achieve longer-term goals (such as checking Facebook instead of doing work or eating the cake a colleague brought in instead of an apple).

To explore that link, we surveyed 229 employees from various organizations to learn what they typically did on their way to work and discovered that those who scored high on measures of self-control tended to use the time to engage in productive planning—what we call *work-related prospection.* "I think about what I will do when I get into the office," one participant told us. "I try to plan out what things I will accomplish for the day."

Our final step was to investigate whether everyone—not just the most disciplined people—could benefit from the same exercise. We recruited 443 full-time US workers with commutes of 15 minutes or more for a four-week study. In the first two weeks, participants received daily prompts that allowed us to measure how much work-related prospection they did during their morning travel. As before, we found that those who did the most planning were better able to handle longer commutes. In the second two weeks, we randomly assigned the same participants to one of four conditions. In a daily text message that arrived 15 minutes before they typically left for work, we asked some of them to engage in work-related prospection as they traveled, some to engage in relaxing thoughts and activities, and others to do both. A quarter of the participants received a text message that did not contain any particular prompt. We found that only employees in the first group—those asked to engage in productive planning and nothing else—reported feeling more satisfied with their jobs than they had prior to the intervention. This finding held regardless of their natural propensity for self-control, as measured at the start of our study.

So this is a simple, straightforward strategy available to everyone. Simply ask yourself: What steps can I take today and during this week to accomplish my work and career goals? How can I be more productive?

Find Your "Pocket of Freedom"

As you sit in traffic, wait for a delayed bus, or stand in a crowded subway car, you may feel you have little control over your commute. But you can temper that frustration by focusing on what you *can* control: how you spend your time during the trip. We've already talked about rituals and planning, but think also about activities that you enjoy, such as listening to music, catching up on podcasts, or reading books. We borrowed the phrase "pocket of freedom" from Adela, the great-aunt of one of us (Jon), whose early adult years were spent in various Polish ghettos during the Nazi occupation. No matter how hungry, tired, or frightened she was, she devoted one hour each night to a creative activity with her niece—a practice that, she later noted, helped her persevere. Though the stakes in a commute to work are much less significant, you, too, can make the time more bearable by thinking of it as an opportunity to pursue your passions. Beyond passive media consumption, you might use the time to learn a new language via audiotape or, if your hands are free, take up a new hobby, such as drawing or knitting.

This advice is supported by research that shows a correlation between higher levels of autonomy and greater well-being, satisfaction, and productivity, and lower levels of stress. For example, John Trougakos of the Rotman School of Management and his colleagues discovered that employees who could decide where, when, and how to spend their lunch breaks felt more replenished by them than those who had no choice.

So try to tune out the negatives of commuting and concentrate on the opportunity to express yourself and recharge.

Share the Spirit

So far, we have explored how you can improve your commute by dedicating it to solitary pursuits. But one of the downsides of long travel to and from work is that it can be lonely. In fact, when Harvard political scientist Robert Putnam studied the issue, he found that for each extra 10-minute period that people spent commuting, they had 10% fewer social connections, which led to greater isolation and unhappiness. We recommend preempting that problem by using your commute to reach out to others.

Most research on the psychological benefits of social connection focuses on relationships with family or close friends. But according to studies conducted by behavioral scientists Nicholas Epley of the University of Chicago and Juliana Schroeder of the University of California at Berkeley, talking to strangers can improve well-being for commuters. Epley and Schroeder went to a train station, recruited more than 200 people, and randomly assigned them to one of thrcc groups. Some were instructed to connect with a fellow rider, others were asked to keep to themselves, and the rest were told to behave as they normally would. Although participants predicted that their ride would be more enjoyable if they sat in solitude, the research team found that the opposite was true: Those who were asked to engage in conversation had a more positive commuting experience and felt no less productive.

Another study, from the New Cities Foundation, found that even using social sharing apps, such as Waze, can trigger this effect and reduce drivers' transport-related stress.

So think about how you might be more social as you commute. If you take public transportation, consider removing your headphones and flouting the unwritten rule against chitchat. If you drive, put your phone on speaker and call a friend, ask a neighbor who works near you to ride with you, or try an app, such as Sluglines, that helps coordinate casual carpooling. If you live in a city that has Uber, choose uberPOOL (which will connect you with strangers) over uberX (where you ride by yourself). And if you're on a company-provided shuttle, as is often the case for Silicon Valley tech companies, talk to your seatmate.

Reduce Your Commute

If you've done all you can to make the most of your existing commute but it's still causing you stress, making you unhappy, and killing your productivity, there is another option. Reduce it.

This starts with the decisions you make about where to live and work. Most people overweight the upside of traveling a greater distance—a job with a higher salary, for example, or a larger house in a nicer neighborhood—while underweighting the downsides of commuting. We call this commuter's bias. To test it, we conducted an as-yet-unpublished study in which we asked more than 500 full-time US employees from a wide range of industries to choose between two scenarios: Job 1, with a salary of $67,000 a year and a commuting time of 50 minutes, and Job 2, with a salary of $64,000 and a commuting time of 20 minutes. Everything else would be equal: the neighborhood where they lived, the advancement opportunities at work, and how much they would enjoy the role. A full 84% of our participants chose Job 1, thus expressing a willingness to forfeit one hour each workday to their commute—250 hours per year—in exchange for just $3,000. That's $12 an hour of commuting time—

less than half their hourly rate at work! We checked to see whether participants could do this math, and they could. Their responses simply reflected an inability to fully appreciate the psychological, emotional, and physical costs of longer travel times.

If you're considering a new job or looking for a new apartment or house, we encourage you to resist this bias. Carefully consider the downsides of a long commute before committing yourself to one.

One way to reduce your commute without switching jobs or moving is to occasionally work from home or at a place closer to home, such as the shared offices provided by companies like WeWork. Telecommuting is becoming increasingly common: In 2015, 24% of US workers did some or all of their work at home, according to the US Census, and research from Global Workplace Analytics suggests that regular telework has more than doubled over the past decade. Studies have also shown that people who have the choice of working from home on some days are more productive and happier than those who don't. In a field experiment conducted at the Chinese travel agency Ctrip, Stanford economist Nick Bloom and his colleagues found that employees randomly assigned to work from home accomplished 13% more than those assigned to work from the office, reported being more satisfied with their jobs, and were 50% less likely to quit their organizations. So if your employer allows flexible work, and you think your boss and teammates would be amenable to your telecommuting, try it one day a week or a few days a month.

Conclusion

Most people who have long commutes feel like helpless victims enduring a necessary evil. As a result, they arrive at their jobs and homes depleted, and their performance and well-being suffer. But it is possible to improve your commute by turning it into a more positive experience and, when possible, reducing it.

Francesca Gino is a behavioral scientist and the Tandon Family Professor of Business Administration at Harvard Business School. She is the author of the books *Rebel Talent: Why It Pays to Break the Rules at Work and in Life* and *Sidetracked: Why Our Decisions Get Derailed, and How We Can Stick to the Plan.* Twitter: @francescagino. **Bradley Staats** is an associate professor at the University of North Carolina's Kenan-Flagler Business School. Follow him on Twitter at @brstaats. **Jon Jachimowicz** is a PhD candidate at Columbia Business School. In his research, Jon investigates the antecedents, perceptions, and consequences of passion for work, the impact of work-related nonwork behavior, such as commuting and workplace distractions, and the influence of environmental forces on judgments and decisions. His website can be found at jonmjachimowicz.com. **Julia Lee** is an assistant professor of Management & Organizations at the University of Michigan's Ross School of Business. **Jochen Menges** is the chair of Human Resource Management and Leadership, University of Zurich.

CHAPTER 24

Get Better Sleep

by Ron Friedman

How much sleep did you get last night? If the answer is "not enough" you're hardly alone. According to Gallup's estimates, almost half the people you'll run into today are suffering from some level of sleep deprivation.

We often dismiss a little morning fatigue as an inconvenience, but here's the reality. Missing sleep worsens your mood, weakens your memory, and harms your decision-making all day long. It scatters your focus, prevents you from thinking flexibly, and makes you more susceptible to anxiety. (Ever wonder why problems seem so much more overwhelming at 1 a.m. than in the first light of day? It's because our brains amplify fear when we're tired.) When we arrive at work sleepy, everything

---

Adapted from "How to Spend the Last 10 Minutes of Your Day" on hbr.org, November 10, 2014 (product #H012NM).

feels harder and takes longer. According to one study, we are no more effective working sleep-deprived than we are when we're legally drunk.

It's worth noting that no amount of caffeine can fully compensate for lack of sleep. While a double latte can make you more alert, it also elevates your stress level and puts you on edge, damaging your ability to connect with others. Coffee can also constrain creative thinking.

To perform at our best, our bodies require rest—plain and simple. Which underscores an important point: On days when we flourish, the seed has almost always been planted the night before.

Since most of us can't sleep later in the morning than we currently do, the only option is to get to bed earlier. And yet we don't. Why? The reason is twofold. First, we're so busy during the day that the only time we have to ourselves is late in the evening—so we stay up late because it's our only downtime. Second, we have less willpower when we're tired, which makes it tougher to force ourselves into bed.

So, how do you get to bed earlier and get more sleep? Here are a few suggestions, based on goal-setting research.

Pick a Bedtime

Start by identifying an exact time when you want to be in bed. Be specific. Trying to go to bed "as early as possible" is hard to achieve because it doesn't give you a clear idea of what success looks like. Instead, think about when you need to get up in the morning and work backward. Try to give yourself eight hours, meaning that if you'd like to be up by 6:45 a.m., aim to be under the covers no later than 10:45 p.m.

Identify Time-Sinks

Next, do a nighttime audit of how you spend your time after work. For one or two evenings, don't try to change anything—simply log everything that happens from the moment you arrive home until you go to bed. What you may discover is that instead of eliminating activities that you enjoy and are keeping you up late (say, watching television between 10:30 and 11 p.m.), you can start doing them earlier by cutting back on something unproductive that's eating up your time earlier on (like mindlessly scanning Facebook between 8:30 and 9 p.m.).

Create a Ritual

Once you've established a specific bedtime goal and found ways of rooting out time-sinks, turn your attention to creating a pre-sleep ritual that helps you relax and look forward to going to bed. A major impediment to getting to sleep on time is that when 11 p.m. rolls around, the prospect of lying in bed is not as appealing as squeezing in a quick sitcom or scanning tomorrow's newspaper headlines on your smartphone. Logically, we know we should be resting, but emotionally we'd prefer to be doing something else.

To counteract this preference, it's useful to create an enjoyable routine, one that both entices you to wind down and enables you to go from a period of activity to a period of rest. The transition is vital. Being tired simply does not guarantee falling asleep quickly. First you need to feel relaxed. But what relaxes one person can exasperate another. So I'll offer a menu of ideas to help you identify a bedtime ritual that's right for you:

- **Read something that makes you happy.** Fiction, poetry, graphic novels: whatever sustains your attention without much effort and puts you in a good mood. (Warning: Never read anything work-related in bed. Doing so will make it more difficult for you to associate your bed with a state of relaxation.)

- **Lower the temperature.** Cooler temperatures help us fall asleep and make the prospect of lying under the covers more appealing. The National Sleep Foundation recommends keeping your thermostat between 60 and 67 degrees overnight.

- **Avoid blue light.** Exposure to blue light—the kind emanating from our smartphones and computer screens—suppresses the body's production of melatonin, a hormone that makes us feel sleepy. Studies show that reducing exposure to blue light, either by banishing screens before bedtime or by using blue light–blocking glasses, improves sleep quality.

- **Create a spa-like environment.** Establish a tranquil environment with minimal stimulation. Dim the lights, play soothing music, light a candle.

- **Handwrite a note.** One of the most effective ways of boosting happiness is expressing gratitude. You can experience gratitude while writing a thank-you note to someone you care about, or privately, by listing a few of your day's highlights in a diary.

- **Meditate.** Studies show that practicing mindfulness lowers stress and elevates mood.
- **Take a quiet walk.** If the weather's right, an evening walk can be deeply relaxing.

Experts recommend giving yourself at least 30 minutes each night to wind down before attempting to sleep. You might also try setting an alarm on your smartphone letting you know when it's time to begin, so that the process becomes automatic.

However you choose to use the time before bed, do your best to keep this time free of negative energy. Avoid raising delicate topics with your spouse, and don't even set your morning alarm right before going to bed—it will just get your mind thinking about the stresses of the next day. (Instead, reset your alarm for the following morning right when you wake up.)

And finally, keep a notepad and a light-up pen nearby. If you think of something you need to do the next day, jot it down instead of reaching for your smartphone. Do the same for any important thought that pops into your head as you are trying to fall asleep. Once you've written it down, you'll find it's a lot easier to let go.

Ron Friedman, PhD, is an award-winning psychologist and the founder of ignite80, a company that teaches leaders practical, evidence-based strategies for working smarter and creating thriving organizations. He is the author of *The Best Place to Work: The Art and Science of Creating an Extraordinary Workplace*, and frequently delivers keynotes and workshops on the science of workplace excellence.

CHAPTER 25

Don't Take a Bad Day Home with You

by John Baldoni

Feeling frustrated at work—especially late in the day, when you're worn out? Right before you go home, do something that comes easily to you.

That advice was given to my daughter, a drop-in diver in a collegiate program. One day she had hit a wall and was about to head home when her coach pulled her aside and said, "Instead of leaving in a state of frustration, why don't you finish practice with a dive you *know* you do well?" My daughter followed her suggestion and left feeling much better about herself and her abilities.

Adapted from content posted on hbr.org, August 9, 2010.

And that's exactly what we nondivers need to do. Things inevitably go wrong on the job because of our own or others' mistakes or failed systems or processes. Whatever the cause, tension builds. To prevent that stress from following you out the door and ruining your evening, dissipate it before you wrap things up.

Whether it's sending off a routine report or replying to a few straightforward emails, cross an item off your to-do list. Pick something that doesn't require much thought. This type of activity tends to slow your heart rate and give you a sense of ownership of what you're doing.

Once you've completed the task—and are hopefully feeling better—exit promptly. Do not check your email one last time. Do not linger to see who else is hanging around. Just leave—gracefully, and with a smile on your face. The onerous work will be there tomorrow, but for the moment, flush it from your memory. For now, just go.

Of course, this won't always work. Sometimes you'll still leave exasperated. And if that happens more often than not, you probably have a larger problem to solve. You may need to find a new position, a new employer, or even a new line of work. But for the occasional bad day, doing one more dive that makes you feel good about yourself before you head home can help you leave your frustrations behind you.

John Baldoni is a leadership consultant, coach, and speaker. His newest book is *The Leader's Pocket Guide* (AMACOM, 2012).

Index

anxiety, 213, 223. *See also* self-care
apologizing, 179. *See also* relationships
aspirations, 44–46. *See also* priorities
authenticity
  identities and, 60
  self-care and, 186
  Total Leadership and, 8, 14
autonomy, 67, 70. *See also* decision-making
avocational domain, 44. *See also* domains

Baldoni, John, 237–238
Bayer Healthcare, 108–109
bedtime, 232–233. *See also* self-care
belonging, the need for, 149. *See also* friendships
bereavement leave, 142. *See also* flexible work arrangements
blue light, 234. *See also* sleep
boundaries
  days off and, 95–99. *See also* time management
  experimenting with, 22–23
  flexible working arrangements and, 134–135
  managing around identities, 59–60
  parenting and, 173
  part-time work and, 113–114
  personal crises and, 139
  rituals and, 123–124
  setting, 73–82
  time budgets and, 74–76
  untouchable days and, 89–94
  between work and play, 173
brainstorming
  possibilities in Total Leadership exercise, 9
  for two-career couples, 156–160
breaks, 204, 212. *See also* self-care
Bregman, Peter, 83–88
"The Broken Compass," 172. *See also* parenting
budgeting time. *See* time management

caffeine and sleep, 232. *See also* sleep
career development, 44
  experiment design for, 21

career development (*continued*)
flexible work arrangements and, 126–128
friendships and, 147–152
personal crises and, 137–143
questions to ask about, 63–71. *See also* time management
for two-career couples, 153–160. *See also* relationships
Caza, Brianna, 53–62
champions, flexible work arrangements and, 113, 124–126. *See also* flexible work arrangements
coffee and sleep, 232. *See also* sleep
cognitive health and exercise, 215–220. *See also* self-care
communication
about personal crises, 137, 138–141
about time off, 170–171
asking for help, 79–80, 140–141
with family when work gets crazy, 178–181
flexible work arrangements and, 126–128
learning to say no and, 83–88
in meaningful relationships, 150–151
with school personnel, 173–174
taking time off from, 133–134
time management for, 78
during your commute, 226–228
commute time, 221–230. *See also* self-care
connections. *See also* relationships
between identities, 56–58
consequences, 178–179. *See also* relationships
context, 178. *See also* relationships
control, 67, 70, 225–226. *See also* decision-making
Corwin, Vivien, 111–129
cost vs. benefit analysis, 48–49. *See also* decision-making
coworkers
asking for help from, 140–141, 142–143
getting input from about flexible work arrangements, 105–106
part-time work and, 119–120
sharing/communicating with, 139–140
Creary, Stephanie, 53–62
creativity and innovation
coffee and, 232
connections between identities and, 57–58
part-time work and, 124–125
Total Leadership and, 14
two-career couples and, 156–160
untouchable days and, 90, 92
crises, personal, 137–143

days off, 95–99. *See also* time management
development, personal, 108–109
decision-making
about commuting, 228–229
about taking on new work, 63–71
cost-benefit analysis for, 48–49
determining whether you have a choice and, 67, 70

for dual-income couples, 155–156
investment/opportunity costs and, 47–48
life dimensions and, 43–46
motivation in, 64–66
needs vs. wants and, 46–47
small-wins approach to, 29–31
time management and, 74
Total Leadership approach to, 7–31
trade-offs in, 41–51
values alignment and, 66–69
values assessment and, 46–51
worksheet for, 68–69
dimensions of life, 7–31, 43–46
experimenting with, 9–10, 15–26
listed, 7
making trade-offs among, 7-8
measuring progress in, 26–29
small wins in changing, 29–31
Total Leadership process for, 8–31
domains, 7–13, 43–44
brainstorming and experimenting around, 9–10, 15–26
leadership and, 11–12
measuring progress in, 26–29
reflecting on, 9
Dowling, Daisy Wademan, 161–175
dual-income couples, 153–160. *See also* relationships
Dutton, Jane, 138, 139

Edmondson, Amy, 187
effects, minimizing negative, 179. *See also* relationships
efficiency, 121, 165
80/20 rule, 78. *See also* decision-making
email, 78, 133–134. *See also* time management
energy, 189, 202. *See also* self-care
engagement
intrinsic vs. extrinsic motivation and, 65
Total Leadership and, 19–20
workaholics and, 199–207
environment
changing when you're not at work, 212–213
self-care and, 188–189
for sleeping, 234–235
time off and, 99
Epley, Nicholas, 227–228
equality vs. equity, 106. *See also* flexible work arrangements
exercise, 215–220. *See also* self-care
expectations, 180. *See also* relationships
determining reasonableness of, 74
realistic, 12
experiments
adapting, 24–26
around flexible work arrangements, 105
around priorities, 36–37
choosing, 23–26
evaluating, 26–29
how to design, 17–21
identifying possibilities for, 16–23
metrics for, 26–29
most fruitful, 36–37
in Total Leadership, 9–10, 11–12, 15–26

Facebook, 142. *See also* bereavement leave
family, 44
  parenting and, 161–175
  when work gets crazy, 177–181
family study hall, 172–173. *See also* parenting
flexible work arrangements, 101–143
  adjusting, 106–107
  benefits of, 104, 229
  bereavement leave, 142
  business case for, 119–121
  case studies on, 107–109
  champions for, 113, 124–126
  confidence and, 115
  for decompression, 98–99
  defining what you want in, 104–105
  employee retention and, 229
  experimenting with, 20, 22, 105
  5% solution in, 167–168
  getting team input on, 105–106
  job satisfaction and, 229
  options in, 104–105
  organizational benefits of, 106, 229
  organizational discomfort with, 128
  part-time, 111–129
  personal crises and, 137–143
  productivity and, 229
  reasons for seeking, 117
  reducing your commute and, 229
  selling to the boss, 167
  setting boundaries in, 134–135
  setting working hours in, 132–133
  staying focused in, 131–136
  structuring for success, 133–134
  telecommuting, 229
  Total Leadership and, 20
  untouchable days and, 89–94
  winning support for, 103–110
flow states, 92, 203
focus
  Total Leadership and, 19
  on what to do instead of working, 210–212
  working from home and, 131–136
Ford Motor Company, 107–108, 222
"The Four-Way View Test" (Friedman), 33–37
Friedman, Ron, 215–220, 231–236
Friedman, Stewart D., 2, 7–31, 33–39, 104, 106, 177–181
friendships, 9, 147–152. *See also* relationships
  experiments in improving, 17, 37
  life dimension of, 44
  saying no in, 86
  time management and, 46, 68, 92, 98
  Total Leadership approach and, 8
  working from home and, 131–132
  work overload and, 73
Frost, Peter J., 111–129
frustration
  commuting and, 225–226
  taking a bad day home with you, 237–238
  untouchable days and, 92

fulfillment
  long-term, 43
  Total Leadership and, 8, 11

Gallo, Amy, 103–110, 137–143
Gino, Francesca, 221–230
goals
  accepting limits around, 42–43
  aspirational, 44–46
  having it all and, 41–51
  negative, 210–211
  for nonwork time, 210–212
  in parenting, 174–175
  sequential pursuit of, 50–51
  sustainable change toward, 36–37
gratitude, 234–235. *See also* self-care
grief, 141–142. *See also* flexible work arrangements

habits, 211. *See also* self-care
harmonious passion, 202. *See also* workaholics
having it all, 7–31, 41–51
  assessing value and, 46–51
  idea of in brief, 7–8
health and well-being, 44. *See also* self-care
  exercise and, 215–220
  loving your work and, 197–201
  sleep and, 231–236
  workaholics/working long hours and, 195–201
help, asking for, 79–80, 140–141
hobbies, 205. *See also* self-care
holistic approaches
  creating connections between identities, 56–58
  Total Leadership and, 14
homework, 172–173. *See also* parenting
Houlder, Dominic, 66, 68–69

identities
  authenticity and, 60
  boundaries between, 59–60
  complements among, 57
  creating connections between, 56–57
  either/or thinking about, 55–56
  how we act out, 58–61
  leveraging connections between, 57–58
  multifaceted, 54–55
  overinvesting in one, 53–54
integration, 2, 4
integrity, Total Leadership process and, 14
interior monologues, 203. *See also* self-care
intrusive thoughts, 211–212. *See also* self-care
investment costs, 47–48. *See also* decision-making
isolation, 90–91, 226–227. *See also* untouchable days

Jachimowicz, Jon, 221–230
job shares, 107–108. *See also* flexible work arrangements
judgment, 186

Kaufman, Scott Barry, 202–205
Kreamer, Anne, 138–139, 140, 141

Lawrence, Thomas B., 111–129
leadership, 11. *See also* Total Leadership process
leaves of absence, 141–142. *See also* flexible work arrangements
life dimensions. *See* dimensions
limits. *See also* boundaries
  accepting, 42–43
  explaining your, 135
  time budgets and, 80–81
loving your work, 197–201. *See also* workaholics

managing time. *See* time management
Markle, Meghan, 55–56. *See also* identities
Markman, Art, 209–214
material domain, 44. *See also* domains
meditation, 235. *See also* self-care
Menges, Jochen, 221–230
metrics
  for experiments, 17, 26–29
  in Total Leadership process, 10
micro-vacations, 96–99. *See also* self-care; time management
mindfulness, 235. *See also* self-care
mindset, 204–205, 222–223
minimizing negative effects, 179. *See also* relationships
money
  regrets related to, 148–149
  self-care and, 187
money, as motivator, 65. *See also* motivation
motivation
  identifying your, 65
  intrinsic vs. extrinsic, 64–66, 206
  personal crises and, 139
  workaholism and, 206
  for work changes, 64–66

needs vs. wants, 46–47, 138, 149, 204–205. *See also* decision-making
negative effects, minimizing, 179. *See also* relationships
networking, 127–128. *See also* relationships
no, saying, 83–88

obligations, 64, 67, 70. *See also* priorities; decision-making
  learning to say no and, 83–88
obsession, 193–207. *See also* workaholics
obsessive passion, 202. *See also* passion
opportunities, missing out on by saying no, 86. *See also* no, saying
opportunity costs, 47–48. See also decision-making
organization
  experimenting with time, 22. *See also* time management
  for experiments, 17–18

parenting, 161–175
  building a village for, 164
  crisis management and, 165–166

dealing with teachers/administrators and, 173–174
delegating and, 165
in dual-career couples, 153–160
efficiency in, 165
homework and, 172–173
flexible work arrangements and, 117, 142–143, 166–168
identity and, 58–59
of school-age kids, 169–175
shifting your mindset from, 222–223
time management and, 69, 92, 169–175
Total Leadership approach in, 8, 37, 44
vision in, 163–164
part-time work. *See also* flexible work arrangements
approaches to, 113
business case for, 119–121
informal arrangements for, 113
respect and, 113–116
strategies for successful, 111–129
Pasricha, Neil, 89–94
passion, 197–205. *See also* workaholics
performance
exercise and, 218
self-care and, 187
Total Leadership and, 13
Total Leadership process and, 11–14
personal crises, 137–143. *See also* flexible work arrangements
planning
experimenting with, 22
for experiments, 17–18
parenthood and, 165–167
for relationships, 150–152
for two-career couples, 153–160
for untouchable days, 90
for volunteer commitments, 171
during your commute, 223–225
pockets of freedom, 225–226. *See also* commute time
power couples, 158–159. *See also* relationships
priorities, 4. *See also* decision-making
assessing value among, 46–51
comparing time allocation on, 33–39
exercise as, 217
experiments for, 36–37
flexible work arrangements and, 117–119
focusing on important, 33–39
learning to say no and, 84
looking for gaps between actions and, 35–36
relationships as, 151–152
privacy, 138–139. *See also* personal crises
proactive mentality, 206. *See also* workaholics
productivity, 188–189
commuting and, 223–225
working from home and, 229
purpose, 178. *See also* relationships

quitting, 166–167. *See also* parenting

racial identity, 55–56. *See also* identities
Ramarajan, Lakshmi, 53–62
reading and sleep, 234. *See also* sleep
reflection
  experimenting with, 22
  for experiments, 17
  in Total Leadership, 9
regret, 148–149. *See also* relationships
Reid, Erin, 53–62
relationships, 44, 145–181
  acting out our identities and, 58–61
  being too busy for, 147–152
  benefits of, 148
  challenges of today, 149
  commuting and, 226–228
  exercise and, 219–220
  experiments and, 18–19
  flexible work arrangements and, 127–128
  regret about, 148–149
  self-care and, 188
  steps toward more meaningful, 150–152
  time off for, 98
  Total Leadership and, 8, 18–20
  unhealthy, 201
remorse, 179. *See also* relationships
respect, 113–116, 126–128. *See also* flexible work arrangements
Rhimes, Shonda, 53–54. See also decision-making
risk assessment, 139. *See also* boundaries
rituals
  commuting and, 223
  flexible work arrangements and, 122–124
  sleep, 233–235
Roese, Neal J., 147–152
roles, overlaps in, 4. *See also* identities
Rothbard, Nancy P., 193–207
routines
  exercise, 217–219
  flexible work arrangements and, 113, 122–124
rumination, 211–212. *See also* self-care

Sandberg, Sheryl, 142. *See also* bereavement leave
satisfaction
  commuting and, 225
  intrinsic vs. extrinsic motivation and, 65
  Total Leadership and, 13
Saunders, Elizabeth Grace, 73–82, 95–99, 131–136
saying no, 83–88
school-age children, 169–175. *See also* parenting
school personnel, 173–174. *See also* parenting
Schroeder, Juliana, 227–228
scorecards, 26–28. *See also* Total Leadership process
segmentation, 22–23. *See also* domains
self-care, 183–238
  defining, 186
  experiments and, 18
  sleep and, 231–236

slipping out of, 189–191
switching off and, 209–214
weaving into your workday, 185–191
self-determination theory, 67, 70
self-image, 202–203
changing how you think about yourself, 55–58
self-management, 190. *See also* self-care
self-neglect, 189–190. *See also* self-care
self-preservation, 190. *See also* self-care
self-sabotage, 190. *See also* self-care
"shoulds," 64, 67, 70, 186. *See also* decision-making
Sinoway, Eric C., 1–2, 41–51
sleep, 231–236. *See also* self-care
socializing, 98, 219–220
social media, 150, 227–228
spirituality, 44. *See also* domains
Staats, Bradley, 221–230
stakeholders
dialogues with, 178–181
in Total Leadership, 14, 15
Stevenson, Howard, 42–46
strengths, 163. *See also* relationships
stress
balancing parenting and work, 161–168
body's responses to, 197
taking a bad day home with you, 237–238
workaholics and, 199–201
Su, Amy Jen, 185–191
success
exercise and, 216
having it all vs., 43
structuring your day for, 133–134
Sull, Donald, 66, 68–69
sustainable change, 36–37. *See also* Total Leadership process
switching off, 194, 196–197, 209–214

taking stock, 5–37. *See also* priorities
focusing on what's important to you, 33–39
trade-offs and, 7–31
teachers, 173–174. *See also* parenting; communication
technology, taking a break from, 212. *See also* self-care
telecommuting, 229. *See also* self-care
ten Brummelhuis, Lieke, 193–207
thought patterns, 204–205
time budgeting. *See* time management
time management
adaptation in, 80–81
asking for help and, 79–80
balance in, 59, 80–81
commuting and, 221–230
comparing actual vs. expected times in, 77–78
exercise and, 217
experimenting with, 22
identifying time-sinks and, 233
making cuts around, 76–77
parenting and, 164, 171–172
for priorities, 33–39
self-care and, 187

time management (*continued*)
time budgets for, 74–78
when work gets crazy, 177–181
working long hours and, 193–207
time off, 95–99, 170–171. *See also* flexible work arrangements; self-care
reducing anxiety about, 213–214
switching off and, 209–214
time-sinks and sleep, 233. *See also* sleep
Total Leadership: Be a Better Leader, Have a Richer Life (Friedman), 33–34
Total Leadership process, 7–31
effectiveness of, 12–13
experiments in, 15–26
four-way wins in, 11–12, 15
in practice, 8–10
principles of, 14–15
small wins in, 29–30
steps in, 8–10
trade-offs, 7–31. *See also* decision-making
assessing, 49–50
in two-career couples, 153–160. *See also* relationships
transparency
about personal crises, 137, 138–141
flexible work arrangements and, 113
learning to say no and, 85
routines and, 122
trust, flexible work arrangements and, 104. *See also* flexible work arrangements
two-career couples, 153–160. *See also* relationships

untouchable days, 89–94. *See also* time management

vacation, 95–99. *See also* self-care
switching off and, 209–214
value assessment, 46–51. *See also* decision making
values
alignment of work with, 66–69
determining your, 66–69
Total Leadership and, 14
vision, 163–164. *See also* parenting
volunteer commitments, 171. *See also* parenting

walking, 235. *See also* sleep
Walsh, Regan, 63–71
weekend trips, 96–97. *See also* vacation
wins
four-way, 11–12, 15–16, 29–30, 34
small, 29–30
Wittenberg-Cox, Avivah, 153–160
workaholics, 193–207
avoiding negative effects in, 201, 206–207
definition of, 195
loving your work and, 197–201
mindset of, 194–195
working hours
long, workaholism vs., 193–207
setting in flexible work arrangements, 132–133
workspace, 188–189. *See also* self-care

Harvard Business Review

Invaluable insights always at your fingertips

With an All-Access subscription to *Harvard Business Review*, you'll get so much more than a magazine.

Exclusive online content and tools you can put to use today

My Library, your personal workspace for sharing, saving, and organizing HBR.org articles and tools

Unlimited access to more than 4,000 articles in the *Harvard Business Review* archive

Subscribe today at hbr.org/subnow

Smart advice and inspiration from a source you trust.

If you enjoyed this book and want more comprehensive guidance on essential professional skills, turn to the HBR Guides Boxed Set. Packed with the practical advice you need to succeed, this seven-volume collection provides smart answers to your most pressing work challenges, from writing more effective emails and delivering persuasive presentations to setting priorities and managing up and across.

Harvard Business Review Guides

Available in paperback or ebook format. Plus, find downloadable tools and templates to help you get started.

- Better Business Writing
- Building Your Business Case
- Buying a Small Business
- Coaching Employees
- Delivering Effective Feedback
- Finance Basics for Managers
- Getting the Mentoring You Need
- Getting the Right Work Done
- Leading Teams
- Making Every Meeting Matter
- Managing Stress at Work
- Managing Up and Across
- Negotiating
- Office Politics
- Persuasive Presentations
- Project Management

HBR.ORG/GUIDES

Buy for your team, clients, or event.
Visit hbr.org/bulksales for quantity discount rates.

Harvard Business Review Press

The most important management ideas all in one place.

We hope you enjoyed this book from *Harvard Business Review*. For the best ideas HBR has to offer turn to HBR's 10 Must Reads Boxed Set. From books on leadership and strategy to managing yourself and others, this 6-book collection delivers articles on the most essential business topics to help you succeed.

HBR's 10 Must Reads Series

The definitive collection of ideas and best practices on our most sought-after topics from the best minds in business.

- Change Management
- Collaboration
- Communication
- Emotional Intelligence
- Innovation
- Leadership
- Making Smart Decisions
- Managing Across Cultures
- Managing People
- Managing Yourself
- Strategic Marketing
- Strategy
- Teams
- The Essentials

hbr.org/mustreads

Buy for your team, clients, or event.
Visit hbr.org/bulksales for quantity discount rates.

Harvard Business Review Press

Notes

Notes

Notes

Notes

Notes

Notes

Notes

Notes

Notes